Common Cents Saving
A Simple, Everyday Approach for Real People

By Vincent Brown
Raymond, ME

Copyright © 2014 Vincent Brown
ISBN: 978-1495381522

Table of Contents

Introduction --- 4
The Proposition --- 9
To Save or Not To Save --- 13
Will A Budget Help? -- 28
Improving Your Tax IQ -- 35
Banking --- 53
Kids and Family - You Gotta Love 'Em ------------------------------ 58
Retirement Plans --- 68
Vacations, Toys and Other Goodies ---------------------------------- 73
Homes and Cars: Life's Major Purchases ----------------------------- 78
Gambling -- 91
So You Think You Need Some Outside Help ---------------------------- 96
A Few Final Thoughts -- 106
Chapter Highlights -- 109
Acknowledgements -- 114

Introduction

As a practicing CPA for many years, my working life involved interactions with thousands of businesses and individual clients with wildly divergent income levels, net worth, goals, priorities and personalities. Those differing personalities and how they processed information to make day to day financial and non-financial decisions was a constant source of intrigue to me and very likely planted the seed for this book. My career routinely involved getting to know people, assisting them in trying to specify their needs and ultimately trying to suggest workable solutions for them. It wasn't long before I became aware that my real challenge was not in coming up with solutions but rather in facilitating their being open to them and able to sustain them in their lives. I found myself sitting down with highly intelligent people who were paying me well for my advice and generally favored and appreciated my ideas but in many cases, we just couldn't make them happen. To further muddy the waters, the success of our efforts seemed to me to be unrelated to their intelligence, wealth, or station in life.

What I have come to believe is that many of us make decisions, financial and otherwise, more on the basis of the inherent human elements of the issue rather than the underlying facts and data. In other words, decisions are often made on the fly, highly influenced by lifestyle, emotion and impulse and less so by logic, common sense and certainly not by the numbers. If true, this results in decisions being made, or not made, for reasons that are potentially unrelated to the financial merit of one course of action over another. I'm not suggesting that this is wrong. In fact, in many cases I believe it is as it should be. At the same time there is not a doubt in my mind that the lack of awareness of this tendency or the unwillingness to at least consider managing it can, and most certainly has, derailed many a family financially and otherwise.

Financial security has always been somewhat important to me in my life and I believe this would have been so even if I had ended up in a profession other than accounting. It wasn't the main thing or the dominant thing but it was a routine consideration in my life. Perhaps naively, I assumed that it was also important to my clients, friends and family and given an opportunity, I'm sure that most would claim that it was. Not surprisingly, as in all aspects of life, there is often a detour or two between the saying and the doing. The heart of the matter is not how important you think it is or say it is, but what you are willing to do to make it a priority in your life and that is the question I will soon ask you to consider. Just how important is your financial security to you?

As was true in my working life, my preference and best efforts notwithstanding, I can't decide that for you. What is important, and why we are addressing it early on, is what your answer to that question is. Moreover, if, like me, you do believe that it is important, can you commit yourself to what is needed to achieve it with some degree of dedication and specificity. In the event that you can, my objective is to help you with the process in some small way by presenting you with a proposition, some suggestions, tools and a lot of motivation. Everything is presented with the knowledge that we are all different, it can sometimes be a struggle, there are a lot of grey areas and we won't always do it right. It has been written assuming that you, the reader, are not necessarily financially astute, or even financially inclined. The only skill I presume you have is common sense.

Everything I propose to you in these pages assumes that it must be about it making sense and having value to you and ultimately is dependent on your ability to make it a workable part of your real life. A former employer simply referred to this concept as a "need" generally defining it as a real and intense desire to take some action to affect change in your personal or business life. This need is not intrinsically valuable, good or necessary. It just is and it is yours for whatever reason. In the case of my former employer, he was astute enough to know that no executive was likely to buy consulting services to fix a problem in his company if he did not personally feel strongly that it was "needed". If it didn't keep the executive up at night, we were not likely to convince him that it was important. So, I ask you to ask yourself, "Do you have a need"? If yes, how strongly do you feel about that need?

My working experience screams out to me that your ability to meet that need, if you have one, will be dependent on your personality, lifestyle and often any number of other external influences that might be lurking about in your life at the moment. My presumption is that we all have multiple needs that come and go at various stages of our life. Further, while most of us generally want financial security, some of us just don't seem to need it or need it badly enough. For those of us that do, we are likely to sense that it will require more than a casual effort to be successful at it, that it is of some benefit to us to live for more than what makes us feel good at the moment, and that we need to make an effort to make good choices. I hope to show you how to address this need and consider these challenges by considering and accepting a very simple proposition.

My proposition is that you consider, understand and commit to what I am calling a "savings bias" which is simply a mindset that focuses on making saving a common sense priority for you. As you will soon see, it involves a lot more than physically putting money aside. This book outlines what I mean by a savings bias, why I think it's important and some down to earth simple tools you can use to make it happen for you. It is a process and not a quick fix.

My suggestions are offered and designed to be implemented as a part of a balanced life, specifically YOUR balanced life, and not in place of it. Every choice, difficult or otherwise, is yours. Only you can decide if you have a need, what it is and how much effort it deserves. Only you can decide how much you are willing to give up now for later. Wimpy, an old cartoon character who was a friend of Popeye's used to say he would gladly pay you Tuesday for a hamburger today. Suffice it to say that Wimpy's words reflect the opposite approach to what I am suggesting. My hope is that you will decide to symbolically forego the occasional hamburger today for the choice of several hamburgers or steak tomorrow. Whatever you do or don't do today may not immediately alter your life but neither will it delay the arrival of tomorrow. The question is where do you want to be when it gets here, remembering what Charles Lamb said "It wasn't raining when Noah built the ark."[1]

My belief is that a commitment to financial security is more important now than it ever was. The economy, like a lot of things, tends to go in cycles. Currently as an American, regardless of your perspective, financial status or political ideology, the possibility of fundamental change in our lives is a very real one with more drastic implications than I can ever recall in my adult life. This uncertainty would seem to be even more motivation to take a more active role in taking financial care of yourself which, I might add, is hardly ever a bad thing under any circumstances.

Some of my suggestions and alternatives may be more opinion or preference than quantifiable fact and if so, they will be noted as such. I will say, however, that if offered, these opinions are not just random suggestions. They are based on many years of experience with thousands of individuals in diverse financial situations and the fact that at the end of the day, we are all just people after all.

---

1 John Shannahan, *The Most Brilliant Thoughts of All Time*, Harper Collins Publishers, 1999, p. 21

Common Cents Saving   **Vincent Brown**

There is also a summary at the end of the book that summarizes the main points of each chapter that you can refer to when the spirit moves you. My hope is that you fill find the following pages beneficial enough that you will opt to do so.

I have heard it said that you will never get rich by saving. In fact, it is a cornerstone of one of those financial seminars currently being presented across the country. It may even be true. I believe that to get really rich you to need to build something, actually or conceptually. In any case, I don't claim that a savings program or bias will, in and of itself, cause you to get "rich" whatever definition you assign to that word. It will, however, alter the way you look at things, cause you to change, or at least reconsider, the way you make decisions and will result in your being financially better off than you would be otherwise. I contend that most people who are successful or have become "rich" employ many of the techniques and approaches we will discuss here to enrich their life with the disciplines inherent in planning, setting goals and making tough decisions.

The Proposition

I am hoping to influence how you approach managing your financial life. Having acknowledged this, it's important that you understand why I think it's important to you and why I believe you are able to do it. You won't find a cure for cancer here but you may find helpful information, a little encouragement and perhaps the motivation to adopt a few basic financial and behavioral techniques that, in my experience, are often overlooked in our everyday life. The subjects, suggestions and disciplines presented are not complex. They are simple, some may say they are even obvious and all are certainly based on common sense. I caution against thinking that simple means easy and more significantly that because something is obvious means that it is always considered. We both know that it isn't. Let's get started and I am sure you will see what I mean.

> **Proposition**
>
> *The first known use of the word was in the 14th century and Merriam-Webster defines it as "something offered for consideration or acceptance".*

Here is my basic proposition to you. Your ability to more comfortably weather life's financial storms, better secure your future and combat the uncertainty that exists in the world today is significantly enhanced if you can commit to taking a pro-active role in the process. I suggest that a commitment to saving, perhaps even making it a bias in your life, is a significant step in the process. I would describe a savings basis as "a reasoned and planned effort to consider and prioritize the long-term effects of the financial decisions you make today in light of your long-term goals while maintaining a healthy and happy lifestyle". Let's state the obvious, namely that it's much easier to say than to do and certainly more involved than setting aside a few dollars from your paycheck in an envelope each pay day.

The benefits of a savings bias or mindset, implemented correctly, will spill over into every aspect of your life. It will cushion the blow when life throws you one of its many unexpected curve balls; it will create discipline and direction in your life; it will help you take better care of yourself and family, make you feel good about yourself; and it will make for a much more rewarding retirement. Retirement may not seem like a critical issue to you now but take it from me it will be sooner than you think. If I could guarantee one positive result of your sharing this work with me, it would be that you move forward very clearly aware of how your ability to manage your choices on a daily basis will critically affect the quality of life for yourself and your family during your life and in those later years when you want to take it easy. Even the least attentive among you will see this as a common theme in most of what I say.

As someone who has just experienced it, I'm convinced that a rich retirement experience is predicated upon providing yourself as many choices as possible whenever it happens. The choices are endless but certainly might include where you'd like to live, how much you'd like to travel, what activities you would like to pursue not to mention the extent to which you will be able to help your family. Other than your health, I would argue that the most important factor in all of these choices is your financial security. Speaking personally, while I could have done more during my working life to better secure myself and my retirement, I am always thankful for those efforts I did make that have made things easier for me now. I wish the same for you.

Unless you are one of the lucky few who is wealthy enough that you will never have to worry about your financial survival, the reality is that financial security isn't likely to happen naturally at least not to the extent that you would like. You are going to have to help it along by creating and owning a plan of savings and managing it. I suggest that a considered and serious commitment to this plan is the key to success or at least a terrific start on it. One thing seems clear to me. If you don't do it I'm pretty sure no one else will.

In addition to suggesting how to do it, I am optimistic that I can help you to want to do it, which of course is the key. I will emphasize the need to maintain a balance in your life through the process. Whatever you do needs to be done in synergy with your real life with some semblance of a smile on your face and this is what I mean by balance. Your chances of success are greatly enhanced if your friends and family support you through the process rather than plotting interventions. I am suggesting that you take an active approach but a reasonable one. One of my former colleagues used to jokingly respond when asked if he was married, "Yes, but I'm not a fanatic about it". I contend that what I'm suggesting is not fanaticism; nor is it an extremely limiting way to live. I will allow for the possibility, however, that it may be one with a slightly different focus from the one you have now. If it wasn't, there would be no reason to expect better results than we've had in the past. For those few of you that believe that any form of imposed discipline, financial or otherwise, is extreme on its face, then that is a challenge we will try to overcome and I believe we can.

If some of what I say speaks to you, it's possible that you may need to consider some change in past tendencies and behavior. Further, you should expect to have to occasionally defer some current gratification for a greater future good. These choices are never easy but always possible and I find it helps if I approach it as a game whenever possible and try to consistently visualize where I hope to be if I am successful in my efforts.

As part of the process we may need to make a few changes starting with some baby steps. Like dieting, trying to quit smoking or just trying to improve your overall health, it starts with assessing your lifestyle now, isolating the most important changes that need to be made, having the will to do it and creating an environment where you can be successful. Samuel Johnson said, "The future is purchased by the past" [2]. This shouldn't be nearly as difficult as dieting or quitting smoking and the effect on your future is equally important.

The truth is that not all of us are equally equipped to make money, make good financial decisions or manage our lives super effectively. If you are generating enough surplus cash that you can't help but accumulate significant wealth and security, this book may have less value for you but the concepts are still valid. In any event, I think it is safe to say that you are in the minority. For those of you whose circumstances are such that you are not generating enough income to cover even your basic needs, then some work needs to be done before you can apply my proposition to your life. Either way, I tried to tailor this book for all of us regardless of our station in life. My basic assumption is a simple one, namely that as good people we have a desire and hopefully a need, to take care of ourselves and our families not only today but in the future and that we know it will take some commitment and sacrifice and will not always be easy.

---

2 John Shannahan, *The Most Brilliant Thoughts of All Time*, Harper Collins Publishing, 1999, p. 32

To Save or Not To Save

We are all familiar with the stereotypical concept of saving. My proposition obviously includes what you have typically understood as savings but only as one element in a much larger lifestyle choice. Consider this choice as a framework, or mindset, through which we process and filter the activities, choices and goals that we choose to make part of our life. Our objective in making these choices is to try and keep our eye on the ball, stay focused on our goals and to try to insure to the extent possible that we process information objectively.

Making the judgment to set money aside in savings almost always involves a choice, often a difficult one that is essentially giving something up today for the hope of something better tomorrow. This is exactly what I am asking you to consider but more so. Consider it savings on steroids. I would like you to consider many of life's choices in advance (planning is not a dirty word) and to try to reasonably consider those choices in relation to your plan for your life. Whether you do it aggressively in a large way and it comes easy to you or you do it passively in small steps and it is a struggle, I believe that we are all capable of doing it and will never be sorry that we did. That's the good news. I certainly can't assure you that it's an easy thing to do because the reality is that for some of us it just isn't.

I am comfortable saying, however, that it will be easier than most of us think it will be. Since it is an activity done solely for your own benefit, it can be embraced naturally and often a small change in perspective is all that is needed to make it work for you.

> **Savings Versus A Savings Bias**
>
> *The act of saving is conventionally thought to be setting money aside while a saving bias involves a mindset that includes budgeting, reducing expenses, managing assets and waste and reflection on important financial decisions.*

When you do it correctly, you will routinely look at ways to save money, resources, time and energy. You will occasionally generate the best results by not doing something or doing something entirely different from what your initial impulse was. You may have to forego a completely logical and pleasurable choice today for the hope of a greater benefit down the road.

Your chances of success increase exponentially if you can do it in a fun way, perhaps by approaching it like a game or at least in a way that is more fun than drudgery. It's a way of thinking, a way of living and if you can apply yourself and be clear about what you are doing, you can easily maneuver around the pitfalls of everyday life and our old nemesis "instant gratification" and feel good about yourself in the process.

Now that we have tried to put a face on what I have been calling the mindset of a savings bias, we will try and focus on presenting some specific saving tools and activities with which to nurture and manage that mindset within your own personal financial reality and to accommodate your style of living.

I find it necessary to digress briefly here. You have likely heard people say that you have to spend money to make money and in some circumstances it is certainly true. Opportunities do present themselves occasionally and at the right time, an investment of cash or other resources can result in significant success and financial reward. That said, our focus here is saving and not the art of investing.

I mention spending money to make money because, in my experience, hasty or misapplication of this concept has routinely drained resources from many of us that otherwise could have been part of our savings. One of my savings concepts is not to spend money foolishly. Too often I have observed that immediately after a decision is made to enter a new business venture, start a hobby or enter into some other life change, this decision is immediately, and often prematurely, followed by large cash outlays. Making a judgment to start anything, regardless of the level of your enthusiasm, need not and should not be a license to throw money at it immediately regardless of how worthwhile it seems at the time. A little reflection and a lot more knowledge can be a valuable savings tool. So try not to be the contractor who borrows a bundle for a new truck and tools before he has his first job, or the would be fly fisherman who loads the garage with equipment before he has ever seen a stream; or the out of shape person who spends more on extravagant exercise equipment than the cost of membership in the gym next door for as long as his interest holds. I won't even talk about boats, campers, ATV's and other toys. If we haven't done it ourselves, we've seen examples of it in back yards everywhere strewn with these unused toys. If you doubt what I'm saying, simply take a look at the classified ads in your local paper and you will get the picture. The point is that saving includes both the commitment to set aside money as well as the judgment and restraint not to apply it unwisely.

Let's assume that my proposition holds some interest for you, at least in concept. The next step is for you to ask yourself a few critical questions. Are you willing and able to commit to a plan of savings in your life that will take money from current earnings and put it into savings vehicles on a consistent and predetermined schedule? Are you willing to live and spend with some limitations? Are you willing to at least attempt to adapt your ongoing spending and lifestyle choices to a greater good? The first and most important step in a savings program is commitment. I'd be kidding you if I implied you could do it simply by "wishing and hoping". The truth is, you can't, at least in any meaningful way. You should also be aware that, if you are to be successful, your commitment must be embraced, or at least accepted, by your spouse or significant other if you have one. It also goes without saying that if you think saving is a temporary fix or backup plan you might consider but only until you win the lottery or hit it big in Vegas you're not quite there yet but read on. I still have hope.

For those of you who are still with me, let's continue. If you are wondering about specifically what we do with your savings, I don't think it's important at this juncture. Will choosing one investment alternative over another result in more or less earnings over time? Of course it will and looking at investment alternatives is a very productive exercise but pales in importance to committing to the concept of saving, especially if you are just getting started. Occasionally, people use their lack of investment knowledge as an excuse not to save. This is unfortunate and shortsighted. Take comfort in knowing that once you start generating capital to invest, even in small amounts, you will naturally evolve to effectively addressing the question of how and where to invest and will do so with more enthusiasm.

To start, set up a savings account (online or at your bank), a brokerage account, an online trading account, buy a small house safe, get an old coffee can, or bury a cardboard box (surely you recognize this as hyperbole of the highest order). The point is to create someplace to consistently put your savings dollars. How you do it initially is not so important but I will assure you that if you implement and maintain a commitment to save, you will quickly start to take a very proprietary attitude towards the funds you have saved and what to do with them. As in almost all things, success tends to lie more in the doing of anything rather than doing nothing waiting for more information. As Elbert Hubbard said, "The greatest mistake you can make in life is to be continually fearing you will make one"[3]. Regardless of the type of account you set up, we will refer to it generically as your "savings account".

---

3 John Shannahan, *The Most Brilliant Thoughts of All Time*, Harper Collins Publishers, 1999, p, 17

The next step is to set a target savings amount. You will need to determine an amount from each paycheck that can be set aside without restricting your ability to pay all of your day to day financial obligations including retirement plan contributions, vacations, entertainment, hobbies, and an allowance for contingencies and emergencies. For this exercise to be realistic your expenditures must consider these diversions as part of your real life. When you have determined what your set aside amount is, transfer it into your savings account on a consistent basis with each paycheck through direct deposit or some other formal and timely procedure to insure that the funds get set aside every time you get a paycheck. Get these funds out of your operating account and into your savings account as quickly and seamlessly as possible. If you hope to save what is left of your paycheck after battling all of life's other financial distractions, you will fail or be significantly less successful than if you commit to setting your savings target aside first. This is a statement of opinion not supported by empirical data but I know it to be as true as the fact that politicians lie.

If it sounds a little childish and unsophisticated, I ask you to consider again my premise that a lot of what works is more about us as people, our behavioral inclinations and the reality of everyday life, rather than quantitative or financial principles. If you don't see the cash you will be less tempted to spend it. My approach is similar to what financial professionals have always termed "pay yourself first" and the notion is analogous to the instruction you hear every time you board a plane. If there is a problem, put your oxygen mask on first before you attempt to take steps to help others.

Before we move on, let's talk about the elephant in the room. If your personal financial situation is such that your income isn't sufficient to cover your expenses let alone provide any surplus, it is fair to say that some more work is needed. There is no need to panic, call the suicide hotline or, heaven forbid, close this book. At the same time, there is nothing at all to be gained and no one is well served by ignoring or obscuring this issue if it is a fact of your life.

First, and forgive me for my slight dose of skepticism, the fact that you may be struggling does not automatically mean that your income is insufficient to cover your necessary expenses. It could very well mean that your income is not sufficient to cover your expenses the way you are spending now. Take a look at this and consider that, in many cases to some degree, most of us have opportunities to consider a change in our habits, lifestyle and spending choices that can result in a real impact on the amount of our disposable income. The changes may be difficult and may not be enough for some of us but history would seem to indicate that not saving is often more about us and less about the math. My observation is not judgmental but a fact borne out by personal experience.

> ### A Few Tips for the Savings Game
>
> *I have suggested that, to the extent possible, you try and make savings a game. Here are a few ideas you might use in that game.*
>
> 1. *After you make the last payment on any loans you may have, continue to write a monthly check for the loan payment amount to your savings.*
> 2. *Whenever you get a pay raise or your take home pay increases for any reason, try to designate most of that increase to your savings account.*
> 3. *When you receive cash from an unexpected or non-recurring source like an overpayment, someone paying you back, a tax refund, bingo winnings or anything else, designate all or most of it to savings.*
>
> *In all of these situations, you are dealing with money you have lived without before you got it, so save it.*

Let's assume that you have been there and done that, looked at the options and made some of the tough choices and you are still coming up short. First and foremost, try and quantify the extent of the problem. In other words, what is the amount of the shortfall? You might be shocked at the number of people who are in this position but can't seem to get around to taking pen to paper in an effort to quantify the problem. It may be an unpleasant reality with no easy solutions but this is certainly no reason not to define the extent of the problem and face it head on. In fact, accepting and quantifying the problem is the first step to addressing it. We can't effectively consider solutions unless we know the extent of the problem in very specific terms. In addition to the obvious possibility of securing additional income through a new or second job you might review your voluntary payroll deductions and consider adjusting your Federal and State tax withholding. A critical review of your day-to-day expenditures is a critical element here as well. The obvious goal is to increase the amount of your take home pay and/or to reduce those expenses that must be paid from it.

Despite all of the above efforts, if you are still stuck treading water financially my advice is to keep working at it as I have seen some pretty miraculous turnarounds in my life, even in my own family. I believe the approaches outlined in this book still have value for you even if not at this moment. The important thing is that you try not to be that person who gives up the fight because it is a difficult one. If you assume that it is a permanent situation from which you will never emerge, it's likely that you will end up being right. It won't be easy but your ability to overcome the obstacles of being in this situation is directly proportional to the effort you make to do so. I honestly believe this and have repeatedly seen ordinary people like us be successful at doing it.

> **What You Need To Retire**
>
> *In an article by Chris Ready from the Boston Globe on Sept. 9, 2012, "People who retire at 67 need to have banked roughly eight times their annual salary to have adequate finances for their retirement".*

Once you have implemented a recurring routine of actually setting aside money from each check, the harder work begins. It involves bringing your savings mindset to other parts of your life. This includes looking at your lifestyle and personal needs with an eye on reducing spending and waste and generally making better choices. For a lot of reasons this may often be the least considered and most underutilized savings tool. It can be an elusive undertaking that may involve sacrifice, a change from what we are used to and often puts front and center the differences in priorities between spouses and among family members. Careless over spending and less than the best choices can be major negative elements in our plans to save but also offer some of the best opportunities for improvement and real substantial savings. These tough lifestyle choices are the ones most subject to your individual personalities and circumstances and consequently less subject to specificity as to recommendations. For the majority of us who can't realistically increase our income substantially, choices regarding expenditures and lifestyle are even more critically important. My hope is that you are aware that there is fertile ground for savings here if you are able and willing to cultivate it.

Many of us are currently lobbying our elected officials to do exactly what I am proposing to you. Not surprisingly they are reluctant to do so but there is a big difference between them and us. They are not dealing with their own funds and the fruits of their own labor. Ironically, while they should feel a greater responsibility in making financial choices on our behalf, they have less to lose for poor choices made. We, on the other hand, will assume all of the responsibility for the choices we make.

As a very minor example, a combination of circumstances recently resulted in my collecting rent on one of my children's homes for a time. The rent never arrived prior to the first of the month. After I called the tenant to inform them that I had not received the check, it would arrive like clockwork a day or two later via overnight mail at a cost to them in the range of $20. Rather than mail the check near the first of the month, the tenant waited for my call and spent $20 every month to send it to me for the sake of a few days. It doesn't take a genius to conclude that whatever the tenant was thinking, it had nothing to do with allocating resources economically and wisely. That significant and unnecessary mail cost would have been better saved or used for entertainment.

We can all generate savings in our own lives by being mindful of the cost of things and what value they bring to us. Or course, there is always the danger of taking things over the top and turning into the family curmudgeon who nags about waste of toilet tissue and paper towels, or who travels all over the county to find the cheapest price for mouse traps. When my children read this it will surely bring back a flood of memories related to my antics over the years. I can just imagine their glee as they exaggerate their memories (for after all, I was completely rational) of my efforts at thriftiness. Nonetheless, I do believe that there are significant opportunities for all of us out there to live smarter and more economically without behaving in such a way that someone writes a Christmas classic about us.

> **American Saving**
>
> *According to the Bureau of Economic Analysis, Americans save an average of 6% of their earnings compared to 30% for China, 14% for Switzerland, and 13% for Germany.*
>
> *The 6% average should be considered in light of the fact that only 41% of Americans save regularly and 43% of American families spend more than they earn.*

Some of us approach and deal with these issues naturally while others not so much. Whether this habit is built in or acquired is up for grabs but my sense is that it can be developed. It takes a strong person to know "when to hold 'em and when to fold 'em".

So latch on to the real issues that can provide savings or benefit to you and try to avoid fighting battles that are un-winnable and/or not worth the fight. If you think I have spent a lot of time talking about savings through reduced spending and waste, you're right. Because I can't define and quantify how it will work for you doesn't mean that there are not real savings there for all us and the reality is that you need not suffer to realize them.

There are an unlimited number of obstacles out there to your financial security and ability to save. They are lurking around every corner, blaring from every TV and mobile device, merely begging for the chance to get your attention. Please allow me the license to exclude emergencies, disasters and bad luck from the list as these are uncontrollable and indiscriminately leveled at us randomly. Of the substantial list of the remaining roadblocks to saving that we are likely to encounter in life, there are a few biggies that I think merit some mention below. In light of my high regard for your intellect and my assumption that you are all blessed with common sense, I have chosen not to deal with some of the obvious ones like borrowing money from the mob, investing in electric cars, windmills, and solar panels (at least for now), financing spring break for your daughter and her friends, remortgaging the house for Christmas presents and weddings, wiring money in response to emails from people in other countries you don't know and standing in line for power ball tickets.

Credit Cards and Credit Card Interest

Credit cards, if you are disciplined and prudent, are wonderful tools for lots of reasons. Use of a credit card allows you to defer using your own money for an average of thirty days from the date you acquire the goods or service, allows you to write one check a month for many expenditures, gives you a permanent record of your transactions, allows you the added safety of walking through life anywhere in the world with small amounts of actual cash in your pocket and some cards even pay you for the privilege. That said, they have, as you may have heard in that classic song, The House of the Rising Sun, "been the undoing of many a poor boy" as well as many families. Caution is the byword here.

Simply stated a credit card is a tool for a well-adjusted grown up and even then should be used with caution. It's fair to say that not everyone is financially or emotionally able to use a credit card correctly and by that I mean able to pay it off every month. It's impossible to generalize but I would strongly suggest that college students might fall into this group. If you aren't in a position to be able to routinely pay off the balance every month, my advice is to strongly consider not using one. Credit card interest is kryptonite to the saver. The combination of the interest charges and the inevitability of the creeping balance is a killer and not something you can work out of easily.

Impulse or Ill-Advised Purchases

For any of you who believe you have never made an ill-advised or impulse expenditure, well, let's just say that I am skeptical. I don't personally know anyone who hasn't owned up to a time or two in their life when they made a financial boo-boo. That certainly includes me and others like me who have never been mentioned in the same sentence with the words impulsive or extravagant. Please don't misunderstand here, I don't deny that some of these choices may have been great fun, did not financially ruin you and you might make the same choices every time given the chance. All I am saying is that we may have all made financial decisions that we questioned afterwards for one reason or another. Whether we are talking about a slight error in judgment or a colossal disaster none of us is immune.

One such purchase I regretted was a brand new jet black Mustang convertible that I bought almost instantaneously right off the showroom floor. I am six four and weighed two hundred and seventy pounds at the time and when car shopping was ultra-conscious of the amount of head and leg room in every car I looked at. When I saw that gleaming black convertible sitting there, the top was down, the handle to the five speed gear shift was staring me in the face and at that moment, comfort didn't seem an important consideration. I have to admit that it was one of the few things I have ever done in my life that my kids thought was cool and without question, I certainly felt cool when I drove it. All of this notwithstanding, it was probably not a wise purchase for me in my circumstances at the time. Would I do it again? At my age now, I highly doubt it. But at the age I was then, well let's just say there were several references in and around my home to a midlife crisis.

No one can say what is right for you. The purchase of a boat, exercise equipment, ATV, snowmobile, a time share, 3D TV, or first class airfare may have been some of the best and most enjoyable purchases you've ever made or maybe they weren't. Either way, I'm suggesting that you think about them a little before the fact in the future. It goes without saying that it is less a concern if you do this once or twice in your life as opposed to it being a lifestyle. As a testament to what can happen, I am the proud owner of an electric drill which I have never used and a ten CD set of oldies which I cannot now locate, both of which I purchased in the wee hours of the morning while I was watching a TV infomercial slightly under the influence. I couldn't find my pajama tops but I managed to locate my credit card and the phone.

After I wrote this section I did a little research and discovered that quite a lot has been written about impulse purchases. Not surprisingly, the marketing folks seem to be aware that it happens to most of us. Much of what I read about the urge to impulse buy coincided with my impressions. I did extract a few random suggestions that I thought I might pass along to help curb the urge. They include that you try to plan your purchases in advance, use a 30 day waiting period for purchases over a certain dollar amount, make a game of avoiding spending, watch less television, be wary of special offers or deals they claim will never be repeated and finally to shop alone. Note that almost all of these suggestions relate more to behavior and discipline rather than to numbers. The real issue is to understand that none of us are immune to these temptations and being aware that they often involve a lure may help us refrain from taking the bait.

Other Debt

Certainly, debt in all its' forms can be a useful tool, a necessary evil and even a fact of life depending on your circumstances. I am aware that every reader of this book may not have income sufficient to take care of all current financial needs and emergencies without ever incurring debt. Every situation is different, people are in transition, emergencies arise and as we like to say in our house, timing is everything. Unfortunately, the fact is that some of us incur debt and are in debt for less than sound reasons. There is little justification for assuming that some future cosmic happening will provide us with the cash we need to pay off debt incurred for something we don't have and want now, especially if it is a non-essential expenditure. With that in mind, take this to heart. If you are contemplating a course of action that involves an investment or expenditure of funds that you don't have and don't reasonably expect to have shortly, that course of action should be avoided or deferred unless there is a compelling and urgent need to warrant it. I'm not claiming that there aren't times when the circumstances warrant the borrowing. I am, however, suggesting that those circumstances occur less than we think and prudence is a wonderful attribute to bring to those decisions. Homes and automobiles can be the obvious exceptions but perhaps not so for Christmas presents, vacations, and toys (including those for us grown-ups). If the most important point I make in this book is to commit to a serious savings regimen, the next most important one may be not to spend money you don't have if it is at all possible.

Some of my most trusted advisors (my kids) suggested that it might be helpful if I could offer some practical tips on how to get out of debt for those of you for whom it is a problem. Frankly, I'm not sure what I could offer that isn't obvious to you remembering that my presumption is that you come to this exercise with common sense on your side. All that I can offer is the use of common sense. Please be judicious about incurring unnecessary debt in the first place. If you are in debt, do all that you can to make paying it off a real priority. Again, with the possible exception of cars and houses, it may be helpful to think of debt generally as a drastic alternative to be used in the case of emergencies only. Please do yourself a favor and think long and hard if you are taking on debt for vacations, Christmas presents, a party, a wedding (you dads know this could be the topic of a separate book) and other non-emergency or personal commitments. Life is full of many horror stories about long, arduous struggles to pay back a loan long after whatever benefit (if in fact there ever was one) we derived from the cash has totally faded from memory. If your mindset is that debt just has to be a part of your life, I would like to say as gently as I can, change your thinking. You are wrong and you will limit your options because of it.

I have an aversion to almost all debt despite believing it can be a great resource in the right circumstances. I have to stop short of saying not to do it, but I have no hesitation in urging you to hate to do it. Finally, if you are already in debt, most especially credit card debt, perhaps some or all of any funds you might otherwise put to savings should be allocated to reduce your outstanding debt as quickly as possible. It goes without saying that a high priority should be given to not using the cards or borrowing more money until you are on sound financial footing. To state the obvious, it is really difficult to maintain financial equilibrium if you are routinely carrying large credit card balances at 18%-24% interest rates.

Waste

We waste a lot of stuff in our society. We all do it and while some waste may be unavoidable, not all of it is and it costs us a lot whether or not we can quantify it. I take a fairly broad approach to what I mean by waste as it applies to our life. The obvious examples are buying too much of anything, using more expensive or name brand products when a much less expensive one would do, buying stuff we don't need at all and a general lack of planning as to how we buy and use things. It is, like many things, a matter of degree, but if you are like me my guess is you could walk around your house right now, perhaps without even opening drawers, closet doors or visiting the attic or cellar to find examples. I am talking about supplies and food as well as hard goods and major purchases

I also include not taking care of the things you own in this category. When we have nice things and don't properly care for them, we are going to spend more than we need to for repair or replacement of them. Without going into my "how to conserve paper towels speech", which my whole family can recite by heart, let's just say that we buy too much stuff, use it frivolously, let a lot of stuff go to waste and generally over do, at least I know I do. All of these activities and choices have a cost associated with them. If we are mindful of this and pick our battles, we will surely achieve savings and I believe we would be shocked if we could quantify just how much that could be.

For those of you who believe a political party, a religion, a course of action or lack of one is going to cause the world, or our little corner of it, to go to hell in a hand basket making planning or saving a waste of time, I don't really know what to say except that I think it's a big cop out. I have heard this theme or a variation of it from a lot of folks, some very close to me. So there is no misunderstanding, I share your concern as there are no guarantees as to what the future holds for us, our children and our grandchildren. The question is whether that is reason enough not to plan. Seems to me that the less you believe you can count on others, especially if you are a person closer to the beginning of life's road than I am, the more you should rely on yourself to try to insulate yourself as much as possible from the army of unknowns milling around in our future, not the least of which are the motives and expertise of those we seem to elect to run things (without question another major topic for another book).

Frankly, if we allow ourselves to be honest, there are already too many of us who do little or nothing because they think someone else will take care of them. Of course, we tend to be discouraged from saying this. And the guilty parties aren't apt to own up to it. It might make them sound selfish or lazy and what a shame that would be. Some will acknowledge that they don't see any need to make an effort to work for something if there are people willing to give it to them for nothing. There may be some perverse logic in such a philosophy, in fact there must be because there seems to be a lot of it going around. My guess is, however, that if you are reading this book this is not your style. My advice is that you do all that you can for yourself because the government can't continue to support those folks for whom it is their style.

So, whether or not you've agreed with everything I've said, I assume that my intent is clear. I define the act of saving very broadly. You will not achieve financial security without elements of saving in your life. At a minimum, we should certainly be able to agree that a savings bias, reasonably applied to your life, is inherently a positive thing involving attitudes and choice. If that is so, allow me to take the leap that making this mindset a part of our life is something we want to know more about so we can better manage our choices. The rest is in the details.

Will A Budget Help?

For some of you, I realize that I am suggesting that you deal with your financial life in more detail or to a greater extent than you may be used to. Part of this process may be an attempt to prepare a budget for yourself. If you want to know if it will help, the answer is yes, I believe it will and it most certainly couldn't hurt. Before I present the case for your preparing a budget, I ask that you take a breath, count to ten or do whatever you must to avoid glazing over and shutting down at the mere concept. Whether you elect to do a budget or not, you can be assured that the concept is simple, the execution of it is very manageable, it will be very helpful to you and I expect quite revealing. In other words, it is a very worthwhile activity which you are totally capable of mastering easily.

One of the first things I asked you to do is to determine a savings target number which is the amount of money you can spare from each pay check to save. A budget is an excellent, if not the best, way to do that. In addition, the mechanics involved in the process will engage many of the positive techniques we are hoping to make part of our financial lives including planning, setting priorities and analyzing and forcing choices among alternatives. Your efforts at a budget need not be sophisticated or unduly detailed. How it's done is much less important than the fact that you endeavor to do it.

A good budget routinely begins with reasonably accurate historical figures, specifically a record of your prior year, or years, financial history summarizing amounts you actually spent for the year on your various activities, both for necessities and non-essential costs associated with life style choices. This financial history can be generated manually, using a spreadsheet or with one of the many inexpensive accounting programs available for your computer. As always, use what works for you. If you can manage it, there are a lot of good reasons to consider an accounting program. There are a number of them out there, some simple and some "nerd-deluxe" versions geared more for professional use. If you are a non-accountant be smart and don't try to overdo. I use QuickBooks, it might be a little more than you need but I highly recommend it. It is not inexpensive but still affordable, and it is well supported, able to be mastered by everyone and very flexible if you ever want to get into more than the basics. Even their basic lower end program has more features and options than you will likely ever use but certainly all that you will need. Because it is arguably the most popular program out there, it's compatible with many other applications and almost all communities boast local experts who offer training and assistance with the program should you need it. It's fair to say that most people don't.

Personally, I don't use the program to actually generate my checks although you can certainly do that. I enter the data from my check register after the checks are written. The attraction of QuickBooks or a similar program is that once you enter your transactions it is very simple (automatic really) to run reports which provide the details of all amounts spent by category for any given period of time and the data is retained forever should you want to review your history or compare activities by years. A little care taken in the organization and classification of your transactions can provide a permanent record of all the information you need to summarize your financial life, plan effectively, throw together a budget and instantly provide all of the information you will need for preparation of your annual tax returns. It goes without saying that effective results with any program are directly proportional to the care taken in organizing, classifying and inputting your information.

So, let's assume that you have summarized prior financial transactions using your method of choice resulting in a summary for the prior year of the sources of the money you received and the totals of how you chose to spend it by category. Using these figures as a starting point, the next step is to look forward to what you believe the next year will look like. The summary of how your money was actually spent in the prior year should be reviewed and assessed critically. Next, adjust those figures for the actual changes in your life as well as changes in your choices to provide an estimate of what this year will look like. And that, my friends, is what a budget is.

If you're with me here, it should be obvious why this is important. Critical assessment of your past choices is the key to making good choices in the future. The accuracy or correctness of your current "going forward" judgments, while hopefully sound and well thought out, is not necessarily the major issue here. What is important is the mere process of attempting, before the fact, to consider alternatives and making your best objective choice with a clear head, also known as setting goals and priorities. While your actual results will not exactly mirror your estimates, it is indisputable that they will be consistently better for having attempted the process. Any prospective choice made objectively, before the fact, without the emotions and other distractions working on you in the heat of the moment, is likely to be a more logical one and consequently more in keeping with your stated goals.

You won't be right every time. You will have to adapt for changes in your life. Your clear-headed objective choices will be routinely subject to the vagaries of your being human and worse, the vagaries of other people being human, and a host of other potential distractions. Knowing the outcome will not be perfect seems to me to be a poor reason not to do anything. George Bernard Shaw said, "If you take too long in deciding what to do with your life, you'll find out you've done it".[4] Is it an inexact science, is it a moving target, are the choices tough and will they involve negotiating differing views and priorities within the family? Yes to all, but the truth is that better planning, an attempt at objectivity and a little soul searching is exactly what we are trying to encourage you to bring to the process. Whatever you do or don't do about budgeting, making a judgment to cut back on areas of overspending, consideration of whether next year is the year the car needs tires or the furnace has to be replaced, or working the numbers so that the family can take that trip to Disney World you've been talking about forces you to set priorities and make judgments in advance. Again, I offer that this is never a bad thing and you will never be sorry for having attempted the process.

Experience leads me to believe that some of you will think that you already do this but in an informal way. Others will view this as a fairy tale approach that is so far removed from how you live now that you can't relate to it. I'm simply asking that you do a little out of the box thinking and consider whether it isn't worth a try. It may be fair to say that having a bias to save may cause us to do nothing more than to think a little harder or differently about our choices. It might even cause us to feel a little guilty about a few of them. There are worse things.

As to the actual budgeting process, generally, given a range of choices, I opt for a conservative approach. Sadly, the odds that we will win the lottery or make substantially more money than expected next year are likely much less than the odds that we will have financial emergencies resulting in higher than expected or unforeseen expenses. This too is an opinion and not supported by empirical data but one that you should have no reason to doubt. For this reason, I tend to be more conservative in projecting income and a little more liberal in estimating expenses. I have included a sample budget as FIGURE 1 in this chapter. It is a one-page summary and will give you an idea of what a budget might look like

---

4 John Shanahan, *The Most Brilliant Thoughts of All Time*, Harper Collins Publishers, 1999, p. 37

and how to structure the numbers. The amounts used in my example are totally arbitrary (made up) and presented for illustration only so don't waste your time trying to relate them to your personal situation. It merely reflects the process I have laid out, namely starting with your historical (last year) numbers and adjusting them for what you know will change or have chosen to change based on your life and priorities. The result of your efforts will be as effective as the accuracy of your historical figures and the care you take in attempting to realistically assess what you are willing to do in the future. There are no right or wrong choices or "right way" to enter the data, just what works for you.

> ### What is a budget and why is it important?
>
> *The following comments were taken from the Duke University personal finance website. "Simply put, a budget is an itemized summary of likely income and expenses for a given period... It is an invaluable tool to help you prioritize your spending and manage your money-no matter how much or how little you have... Planning and monitoring your budget will help you identify wasteful expenditures, adapt quickly as your financial situation changes, and achieve your financial goals... Creating a budget will decrease your stress levels because with a budget, there are no surprises."*

In addition to an accounting program, some comfort level with a spreadsheet program could be very helpful here and in your financial life in general. If you use a spreadsheet for the budget process, for example, replicating it in future years should be a piece of cake, not to mention the ease with which you can update your figures for changes. Spreadsheets are, in general, ridiculously powerful tools and a budget is an ideal application that showcases many of the best features a spreadsheet has to offer.

If the thought of a computer record-keeping program or spreadsheet is so out of character for you that you shudder at the thought but you still see some value in budgeting, be assured that all of this can be done with the same desired results by hand in some form or another. It may take longer and you may have to be more disciplined but of course it will work. All of the principles and approaches offered still apply. Budget or not, you have to do something that provides you with an estimate of your future income, your choices regarding necessary and discretionary expenditures to be made from that income and the amount remaining that you will commit to save.

It goes without saying that your historical records must include all financial activity whether transacted by check, cash or credit card. If your reality is that a lot of your expenditures are made in cash and not just in minimal amounts, you will need to devise a system to capture the nature of those cash purchases or, alternatively, convert them to payment by credit card or check. In a climate of $5 coffees, $12 movies and $6 popcorn failure to record your cash transactions, if they are a substantial percentage of your total expenditures, will certainly affect the accuracy of the numbers. I attempt to use a credit card for everything possible and use very little cash to help ensure that I can more accurately account for what I spend.

Finally, at the risk of repeating myself, please make sure that your projected or budgeted expenditures are realistic and include entertainment, fun and contingencies. You may not budget these amounts high enough but failure to deal with them at all will make the entire exercise a wasted effort.

I've spent a lot of time talking about budgeting but not so much because the budget document itself is important. Personally, I believe it is but of greater value to you is the mindset and tools used in the budgeting process involving the disciplines we have introduced so far. The first is the calculation of how much we are committed to save from our check. Next is the examination of what non-essential financial lifestyle choices we think are important in our lives. Finally is our attempt to manage and control ourselves and our choices on a day to day basis while sloshing around in the trenches of life. In a perfect world, we would deposit our earnings, pay our bills (which would be only essential ones free of frills), and the remainder of our earnings would sit in our accounts available for saving or until we needed it. This may, in fact, be the case for you but I'm confident it isn't for most of us. Something about creating the commitment and discipline to funnel that excess income to a savings vehicle before the fact makes sense as does the discipline associated with trying to manage what we spend our hard earned money on.

Common Cents Saving — Vincent Brown

FIG. 1 - Mr. And Mrs. S. Bias - Personal Budget for the Year 20xx

	Actual Last Year	Prelim. This Year	Adjustments for This Year Notes	Amount	Final This Year
Budgeted Revenues					
Net Salary - Husband	53,200	53,200	Raise - Taken from Stub		58,960
Net Salary - Wife	29,600	29,600	$100/Wk. Raise, Net	4,000	33,600
Fed & State Tax Refunds	1,650	1,650	Adjusted Withholding	(1,000)	650
Gift from Parents	5,000		Won't Receive Next Year		
	89,450				93,210
Budgeted Expenditures					
Home Mortgage	18,000	18,000	One Extra Month Payment	1,500	19,500
Home Property Tax	2,100	2,195	Actual Figure Available		2,195
Home Insurance	843	843	Projected 5% Increase	42	885
Home Utilities	2,352	2,352	Projected 5% Increase	118	2,470
Home Repairs	1,200	1,200	This Year - New Furnace	3,800	5,000
Home Cable TV/Internet	1,500	1,500	Projected 5% Increase	75	1,575
Car Payment - 2nd Car	3,540	3,540	6 Months Left	(1,770)	1,770
Gas Both Cars	3,840	3,840	Assume 15% Increase	576	4,416
Insurance Both Cars	1,350	1,350	Actual Amount Available		1,423
Repairs/Other - Both Cars	1,950	1,950	Normal Maintenance Only		1,950
Food	8,320	8,320	Project 10% Increase	832	9,152
Liquor	1,440	1,440	Plan to Cut Down	(500)	940
School Tuition	9,000	9,000	Will Be the Same		9,000
Other School Expenses	952	952	$100/Month		1,200
Vacation	4,265	4,265	Same Trip/Add 10% to Cost	427	4,692
Entertainment	4,350	4,350	$150/Week This Year		7,800
Grooming - Everyone	651	651	Project 5% Increase	33	684
Vol. Contribs. - Ret Plan	1,200	1,200	Same		1,200
New Computer	0	0	Computer & Software	1,650	1,650
House Supplies	562	562	Project 5% Increase	28	590
Contingency - New TV	0	0	48" Flatscreen	2,000	2,000
Contingency - General	0	0	$100 per Month	5,200	5,200
Total Last Year	67,415		Total Projected Expenditures - 20XX		85,292
Surplus Last Year	22,035		Projected Surplus 20XX		7,918
			Projected Savings Target Per Bi-Weekly Pay Period		305

This is an illustration of a sample budget. Starting with last year's numbers, adjusted for known changes in facts and changes in choices designed to compute the amount to be saved every two weeks from pay.

Improving Your Tax IQ

Hopefully, you've managed to get through the budgeting chapter reasonably unscathed and brimming with confidence to take on the subject of income taxes. Taxes have been a big part of my working life and all those years of preparing returns and working with taxpayers have left me with some very definite, well tested conclusions. First, let me say that for something that affects so many of us, we don't understand it very well at all. Unconsciously or not, we tend to avoid dealing with the subject directly. Our lack of knowledge tends to make the subject intimidating. Maybe our lack of understanding serves some of those in power but for sure it doesn't serve us. This is not a book about taxes and my focus remains on how to help you manage the process of saving. On the other hand, your annual personal tax liability can be a significant chunk of your annual cash expenditures. In fact, contrary to what many politicians and talking heads would like you to believe, the higher your income the larger the amount of your available cash goes to income taxes. Likewise, your payroll taxes also represent a large fixed annual expenditure and the major factor in reducing your gross pay to your take home pay. For this reason alone it's important that you understand these taxes better than you do now not to mention the fact that you can't be affective at efforts to minimize these large annual cash requirements without some understanding of how they work. That is my major focus in this chapter. In addition, I couldn't resist including a few thoughts about income tax refunds and their exaggerated importance to many of us just because I find the subject interesting.

Whatever your thoughts on the subject, you'd have to admit that we have been conditioned to resent taxes, mistrust the IRS and the politicians who administer the law. Coincidentally, as I am putting the finishing touches on these pages, there are allegations (again) that the IRS may have been misused to attack specific groups of citizens for political reasons. I'm sure that over the years most of us have heard horror stories about how the IRS has persecuted people, driven them to the edges of the earth, raped them of their humanity and all of their worldly possessions. It's even possible that some of the stories have a slight element of truth to them. There are evil, ill prepared, malicious, stupid and/or misguided people in every element of society. Some of them may work for the government, some for the IRS and some of them are just taxpayers. The truth is that, in my specific experience, for a group of government employees (and all that that entails) who have too much power, are generally ill-trained and mismanaged, universally hated, routinely lied to and generally treated with more contempt than our worse criminals, they do better than you might think in most circumstances. Many may not be very industrious but neither are most of them malicious. Generally speaking, current scandals aside, if you know what you are doing, stay on top of them and keep your wits about you it is likely that the final result is that you and the IRS will end up reasonably close to getting it right. The other reality is that the vast majority of us will likely never have to deal directly with an IRS agent. The majority of our interaction with the tax authorities is likely to be in responding to computer generated notices relating to any number of issues. In the vast majority of cases these can be dealt with and resolved through correspondence. This of course assumes some degree of knowledge about what you are being questioned about. The bottom line is that a very small percentage of well-meaning, reasonable taxpayers get audited or have issues which require one on one interaction with agents.

Once again, I will endeavor to keep it simple but in the interest of full disclosure, while the material is not really complex, there is a little more detailed information involved and, admittedly, I am predisposed to the idea that you may be starting out with incorrect information that must be undone. My approach will assume little or no tax knowledge on your part with the unintended limitations that there may be some oversimplification and presentation of concepts that you are already familiar with. There is no effort here to make you a tax expert, not even close but rather to get you comfortable with the terms and process so that you feel less helpless on the subject. Whatever your knowledge or interest, this is an important subject and I think even the most tax astute among you may find some useful information here. Before we move on I'd like to share a few thoughts with you about income tax refunds which many of you routinely receive on an annual basis. Regardless of a person's financial condition, receiving a tax refund seems to provide a feeling of pleasure seemingly greater than it deserves. I say that because it is your own money that you are getting back after all. Had you not let the government keep it without interest, you could have had it all along. Whether or not this makes financial sense, I accept that some of us use our payroll withholding as a form of forced savings resulting in the return of our money in a lump sum in our tax refund. This is, in fact, yet another example of a financial choice influenced more by emotion than by spreadsheet. I also know from experience that it is not uncommon for taxpayers to receive tax refunds that are significant in relation to their annual income and can represent the largest dollar amounts of cash that will be received during the year or perhaps in a lifetime. However you feel about the practice of over withholding to accumulate a large refund and whether or not it's the best choice for you, I merely want to emphasize that there are other options and these options may offer a golden opportunity for anyone who wants to get serious about saving.

Common Cents Saving — Vincent Brown

It's possible that you might convince me that overpaying your taxes during the year to get a lot of it back later in a large lump sum as a form of forced savings is not such a bad thing. I am willing to agree to whatever works for you. My experience, however, is that the larger the refund the more likely it is spent long before it is received and possibly long before the return is filed. If any of you doubt this, watch any of the daytime court shows. The majority of the financial dispute cases involve someone borrowing money from a friend or family member and promising to pay it back with their tax refunds. The fact that they end up on the court show means that they didn't pay the loan back as promised but at least they agreed to entertain us with their stories and convoluted logic. Incidentally, it's interesting to note that the litigants on the shows (and many of us) don't call them tax refunds, but rather "tax returns" which just adds more credence to my point that we don't understand our own tax system. Tax returns are obviously the forms you file while tax refunds are the amounts you receive as a result of filing those returns and over paying your taxes.

> ## Who Pays?
>
> *Published figures for the 2009 tax year indicate that the top 1% of taxpayers paid 36.73% of taxes paid, the top 10% paid 70.47% of the taxes paid and bottom 50% of taxpayers paid only 2.25% of all the taxes paid for that year.*
>
> *For the same year, the 400 taxpayers with the highest incomes paid only slightly less in total dollars than the entire bottom 50% of all taxpayers.*
>
> *The average tax refund that year was approximately $3,000; over 47% of people who file returns pay no taxes at all; and over 40% (and it may be higher now) of taxpayers filing returns receive a tax refund in excess of the amount they paid in, if any.*

So, my question is, if we think it is such a good idea to use our tax withholding as a means of accumulating money for a large refund, why do we spend it in advance? What is it about the mere expectation of these refunds that seems to trigger some impulse to use it, sometimes several times over long before we have received it? I suggest that the mere process of trying to formulate specific answers to these questions is part of what I'd like you to examine.

If you choose to have the tax authorities hold your money for you because you are afraid you would spend it were it received in your paycheck, so be it. I can live with that. But if you are spending it long before you get it, wouldn't it have made more sense to keep it in the first place in your paycheck. If you can't get past the need to have the tax folks hold your money for you, then at the very least try not to think of these funds as available to you when you make financial decisions during the year.

One of the financial terms that you may have heard over the years is the concept of "Opportunity Cost". While the actual definition is, in my mind, slightly confusing the basic idea is not. Opportunity cost relates to the financial difference in selecting one alternative over another and the concept has relevance to many of the decisions we make in our lives. When related to the discussion of income tax refunds, it could mean the loss of investment income or the other loss of opportunity to you by not having your own money available to you on a current basis rather than having your taxes over withheld to receive a lump sum refund much later. In other areas consider the opportunity cost concept when looking at alternatives to buying or renting, paying cash or financing and many of other life's financial choices.

Now back to the issue at hand and the purpose of this chapter. It will come as no surprise that there are a lot of different types of taxes including some you have never even heard of. For our purposes, let's limit ourselves to two types of taxes I have already mentioned that affect most of us and arguably have the greatest impact on how much we are able to save, namely payroll and personal income taxes.

Payroll taxes arise in connection with payments of salaries by employers to employees and include employment and withholding taxes. The terms payroll taxes, employment taxes and withholding taxes are often used interchangeably in the current vernacular but they are different and a cursory knowledge of them will be helpful to you. First, they are major players, without question THE major players, in the difference between your gross pay (what you are paid) and net pay (what you actually take home in your check) and secondly they routinely represent a major annual cost to you. Your employer is required to collect, remit and report all of these taxes which has a lot to do with why we as individuals aren't as aware of them as we should be.

Employment taxes represent an incremental cost to both you and your employer as you will see below. All rates and other information are based on laws in effect for 2013 unless otherwise noted. The rates and dollar limits of these taxes often change on an annual basis.

Social Security Taxes (FICA)

As of January 1, 2013 each employee pays 6.2% (it is withheld from your pay) of gross pay up to the first $113,700 per year (the 2013 limit) and the employer also contributes 6.2% of gross pay up to $113,700 (referred to as the match) resulting in a total of 12.4% per employee paid to the government for Social Security taxes. It may be interesting to note that when I got my first job in 1968, the Social Security rate was 3.8% and it was paid only on the first $7,800 earned. The forty five intervening years has seen the rate increase only 63% but the limit on which the tax is paid has risen 1,358% during that same period. This is a non-recoverable cost to every working American with the exception of some public sector employees who are exempt. Why they are exempt is either an unexplained mystery or a travesty if you are living in a rational universe and yet another story for another day. These are your dues paid throughout your entire working life for the right to collect benefits from the Social Security system when you are old enough, assuming of course that our leaders ever get around to figuring out a way to sustain the system.

Medicare Taxes

Each employee (no exemptions) also pays 1.45% of gross pay (with no dollar limitation) and the employer also contributes 1.45% of gross pay resulting in a total of 2.9% paid for each employee for Medicare taxes. There is a new provision in 2013 which requires that taxpayers who make over $200,000 if single and $250,000 if married filing jointly pay an additional .9% for Medicare. This too is a non-recoverable cost and represents your ticket to the Medicare program when you are eligible. Once again, this assumes that steps are taken to maintain the solvency of the system which, like Social Security, is expected to face very real financial obstacles in the not too distant future. It's those damn baby boomers again.

Unemployment Taxes

Unemployment taxes are solely the responsibility of employers, are paid by them and do not cost employees anything; They are mentioned for information only as they do not cost you anything and they do not affect your net pay.

Withholding Taxes

All employers are required to withhold Federal income tax and, where applicable, State and City income taxes from their employees' pay on behalf of the respective tax authorities. How much is to be withheld is calculated from tables provided by tax authorities based on gross pay, frequency of payment, marital status and exemptions claimed. The taxes withheld from you and paid to the tax authorities on your behalf by your employer are formally reported to you and the tax authorities on the annual W-2 form that employers are required to prepare.

While these Federal and State withholding taxes reduce your gross pay like FICA and Medicare taxes, they are different in that they are merely advance payments to the tax authorities of an estimate of your annual tax obligations to them. Whether or not you ultimately owe all or a portion of these "advance" payments won't be determined until your personal tax returns are actually filed. As you know, FICA and Medicare taxes paid are not subject to refund.

If you need more cash to meet your current obligations, to save, or you just want more cash in your pay check currently and you know that you routinely get a large refund, you can make this happen by adjusting your Federal and/or State income tax withholding with your employer. In other words, you document that you choose to alter the withholding that automatically comes from your employers' withholding charts.

How much flexibility do you have in adjusting your withholding taxes? The answer is unfortunately, it depends. Based on the rules you are "safe", which means that you are exempt from penalties and interest to the tax authorities on any additional amounts owed, as long as you have enough total taxes paid from all sources to cover approximately 90% of your tax liability for the year. What I would like you to understand is that for those of you routinely receiving large refunds, you are perfectly within the rules to adjust the amount of income tax withholding from your pay by an amount at least up to the amount of your expected refund, thus providing you with more of your pay on a week to week basis. Sound financial principles would seem to suggest that this is a good idea. If you decrease your withholding and increase your take home pay, will you save or effectively apply the extra cash? Would it be of more value to you and used more wisely than if you receive it in a lump sum as a tax refund? These would seem to be logical, even legitimate, questions even if they may not override that need for forced savings and the false high we feel from getting our own money back. That is completely up to you. I will offer this, however. There is not a doubt in my mind that if you develop a savings bias, your continued focus on your objectives will cause you to think differently about who is holding your money and how it is working for you.

The nuts and bolts of adjusting your withholding within the rules is not rocket science but unfortunately beyond what we can do here. The important thing I hope you take from this is that you may have choices and that those choices can affect your take home pay and available cash to live on and save. Think of it as one of the rules of the game we are involved in while trying to implement your savings plan.

Now, let's talk about personal income taxes but only on a very limited basis. Based on my observations over the years I am convinced that many of us, including our elected officials and others who should know better, don't understand income taxes very well, and maybe not even a little. Without trying to make you an expert I believe I can provide an overview of the basics that will put you a step ahead of most of the population and more importantly, may greatly assist your savings efforts. To start with I'd like you to be familiar with your own return.

I have been intimately involved in the preparation of at least seven thousand personal tax returns over the course of my career for clients spanning the economic strata of society. Other than signing them, I have no way of knowing how many of those clients actually looked at their returns after they were prepared but my guess is very few. For the record, these were predominantly bright, capable and financially secure people. Other than an awareness of the amount of their refund or the amount they still owed, I doubt they did little with their returns other than review my filing instructions, sign and mail them.

There's no doubt they were paying me well for a service, part of which involved trusting me and my expertise to do right by them. The bottom line is, however, that your return is your return and I would argue that you should know a lot more about it than the bottom line. Aside from the obvious fact that you are legally responsible, logic and common sense would indicate that you should have a certain comfort level with the details of your return. Trust is great but "a wishin'" and "a hopin'" leaves a lot to be desired.

I am in no way suggesting that you should be able to prepare your own return though, I expect, some of you might want to try it; neither am I implying that you should know where every number goes on your return or where all the numbers on it came from. On the other hand, I am suggesting that some understanding of how the tax form works and how your return reflects your own financial situation is a good thing. I am not sure how you can try to do any tax planning, consider alternatives or even complain (and don't tell me you don't) convincingly without knowing more than most of us do about the subject. So, let's give it a try using a "flyover" or big picture approach. Stick with me here, it certainly is not beyond you and this may be one of those situations where a little knowledge may take you a long way towards a better understanding of something important to you.

All U.S. residents are subject to Federal Income taxes. Most states and even a few cities levy an additional income tax. The Federal Income tax rules and regulations are the same for all of us but rules and rates in the States and Cities vary. While States have their own income tax departments, the IRS takes the lead in administering most tax compliance and reporting.

As someone who is very familiar with income tax returns, let me say that a personal tax return of 50 pages or more is not at all unusual, even for taxpayers who are not wealthy. Despite this, the basic personal tax return, form 1040, for each and every taxpayer is only two pages long and contains 5 or 6 categories of all of the income, deductions, credits and payments that make up the personal tax system. I will say this again as it bears repeating. Every item of your income and deductions is summarized on the first two pages of your tax return. Every other page and schedule in the return is there to support the first two pages. If you understand the two page form 1040 and the categories it includes, it is the first step to a basic understanding of all of the elements of your tax reality and believe me you will be one of the few that do.

I have included a chart of the major categories included on Form 1040 at the end of this chapter. The following is a very brief description of each of them. You may find it helpful to refer to the chart as you go along. The categories below refer to the major sections or "sub-totals" on your form 1040 but my comments may also refer to the individual line items that make up these totals. Let's look at what makes up your return.

Total Income includes all income or losses (not deductions which are different) resulting from your financial activities during the year. As an aside, you should be aware that almost all income paid to you in any given year is reported to the IRS under your Social Security number and within a year or two of filing your return, a computer check is performed to match up amounts reported in your Social Security number (and your spouse's if it is a joint return) to amounts on your return.

Adjustments to Income (AGI) are certain deductions which by law are given preference and are allowed to be deducted directly from your income by all taxpayers. They are separate from, and in addition to, the standard or itemized deductions. These deductions include payments to an IRA, student loan interest, qualified moving expenses, alimony paid and other specific items so designated as "adjustments to income".

Itemized or Standard Deduction is not a complicated concept but again, one that is routinely misunderstood. Once you arrive at your adjusted gross income (AGI) which is the amount of your Total Income reduced by your Adjustments to income, you are then allowed to deduct *either* a standard deduction or the total of your itemized deductions.

The amount of the standard deduction you are allowed is dependent on your filing status. For example for the 2012 year the standard deduction allowed was $11,900 for married taxpayers filing jointly and $5,950 for single taxpayers. These amounts routinely increase slightly each year. Anyone who files a tax return can claim this standard deduction and automatically does so unless they elect to report and claim itemized deductions instead.

In lieu of the standard deduction, the IRS publishes a very specific list of those expenses qualifying for inclusion as itemized deductions. Any taxpayer can elect to claim itemized deductions but, generally speaking, should never do so unless the total of these itemized deductions exceeds the standard amount you would have been allowed anyway. Because mortgage interest and real estate taxes are included as allowed itemized deductions, having a home mortgage is sometimes the determining factor in whether itemizing deductions will yield a greater benefit to you than the standard deduction.

In addition to home mortgage interest and real estate taxes itemized deductions include personal property taxes, state income taxes paid, charitable donations, medical expenses and certain other specific types of expenses referred to as "miscellaneous itemized deductions". Excepted as noted below, these expenses generally are deductible in their entirety except for some limitations of interest on very large home mortgages and a few other extraneous items. Like many elements in the tax code, things seemingly simple in concept can get complex in application. This complexity can be easily managed or at least better dealt with if you deal with one issue at a time and learn the ropes.

Certain itemized deductions are a little more complicated because they are includable in your overall itemized deductions only if their total amount exceeds some percentage of Adjusted Gross Income or AGI. Unreimbursed medical expenses, for example, can be included in itemized deductions but only the portion of total medical expenses that is in excess of 7.5% of AGI. That means that if your AGI is $50,000 you would need to have more than $3,750 in medical expenses to have the excess over $3,750 added in with your other itemized deductions. Similarly, certain business expenses by employees, tax preparation, financial planning fees and other expenses are includable only if they exceed 2% of AGI.

Exemptions are the final deduction you are allowed and is a flat dollar amount for each dependent you are allowed to claim on your tax return. These exemptions normally include yourself, your spouse, qualifying children and possibly parents and other individuals for whom you provide major support. The amount allowed per exemption was $3.800 in 2012. This concept is a simple one but it may be a referendum on our society today that divorce rates, complex family situations, shared custody and other realities of the times can make determining if you are eligible to claim a dependent child or parent on your return more complex than you would think.

There you have it. You are now at least generally aware of every category of income and deduction that appears on your Federal tax return. These amounts are used to calculate your taxable income which is arguably the most important number on your return other than the actual tax liability. Taxable income is the number on which your actual tax liability for the year is calculated. It is derived from your total income, reduced by certain statutory deductions allowed as "Adjustments to Income", further reduced by either the standard deduction or the total of your itemized deductions and finally by your exemptions. In a progressive tax system like ours, it is also the number that determines the rate at which you will pay income tax.

Your income tax is calculated using IRS provided tables which are different for each filing status. The amount of tax calculated to be paid may be offset or reduced by certain credits, increased by certain other taxes and ultimately will be compared to the payments you have already made resulting in whether you owe additional amounts to the authorities or will get a refund. Simple, right?

My Final Tax Observations

Beware of notices from the tax authorities requesting additional tax payments. Make sure you know it is correct before you pay anything.

Filing an extension to file your tax return does not, in any way, affect your tax status negatively or increase the chance for audit. Millions of extensions are filed routinely every year.

Tax audits are a generally rare occurrence for most of us. Some may be selected randomly, but most are likely the result of some anomaly on the return. If your return is selected and you have been reasonably diligent in its preparation, there is no reason to panic.

Credits (direct offset to your tax liability) are allowed for all, or a portion of, certain designated expenditures including payment of foreign taxes, child and dependent care provided for children, certain energy purchases, and others. Credits are manna from heaven from a tax standpoint because the amount of the credit reduces your actual tax liability dollar for dollar unlike a deduction which merely reduces the amount on which the tax is computed. The important thing to remember about credits is that they are allowed to reduce what income tax liability you have but only the tax liability. Once your tax liability gets to zero, the credit cannot be used although it may be available to you to carry forward to future years. You will see below that there are other even better credits that are termed other payments or refundable credits which are not subject to this limitation.

Other Taxes are other types of taxes that the tax code provides are to be reported and paid as part of your annual form 1040 in addition to your personal income taxes. Some relate to your personal income reported on your return and some do not. These other taxes include self-employment tax, tax (penalties) on early distributions from retirement plans and employment taxes on household employees to name a few.

One brief word about self-employment taxes, likely the most common of other taxes paid on personal tax returns. Self-employment tax is the equivalent of Social Security and Medicare taxes for self-employed individuals. Since self-employed individuals are not employees themselves and do not have employers to withhold and match Social Security and Medicare taxes from payments to them, the IRS requires that the self-employed person pay, in essence, both the employee and employer share of these taxes. The tax is computed on net self-employment earnings and added to the taxpayer's income taxes on the return and must be paid with them. All of those people who operate unincorporated businesses are subject to self-employment taxes on profits which can be substantial as many of you know.

After you calculate your tax liability and adjust it if necessary for credits or additional taxes, you arrive at the total amount you are accountable for paying the tax authorities. This amount is offset by payments made to determine whether you have a balance due or refund.

Payments can include amounts withheld from your salary as evidenced on your W-2 forms, amounts paid directly to the tax authorities as estimated tax payments and another type of credit called a refundable credit. These credits are different from the credits referred to above in that these credits, once calculated, are treated exactly as payments made. They will be refunded to you even if you owe no tax. They include the earned income credit and additional childcare credits to name a few. If the non-refundable credits referred to above are manna from heaven, these refundable credits are the mother lode of taxes. They are so common on tax returns that statistics indicate that over 40% of all returns filed result in refunds to the taxpayer in excess of the amounts of taxes they actually paid. If you think about it, it is pretty staggering. More than forty percent of people filing returns are getting back whatever taxes they may have paid, if any, plus some of the taxes paid by someone else. You don't hear much about this in the political debate on taxation and who is and isn't paying their fair share.

So there you have it. A very broad and general discussion of every category of income, deductions, credits and payments that make up form 1040, the personal income tax return. Please don't misunderstand me here. In no way do I mean to imply that the tax return or the tax rules are simple. In truth, neither is. Without considering a dollar of your income or expenses, just the selection of your filing status and the number of exemptions you are allowed to claim can be very confusing in some situations. There are pages and pages of rules and regulations that cover what may and may not be included on any one line of any one schedule of your return. Because we all have different circumstances, it's impossible to generalize about the complexity of your return. It is fair to say, however, that if these issues are taken individually, the least sophisticated among us should be able to make sense about most issues and there is no shortage of resources available to you for those issues that you can't resolve. In any case I contend that it is advantageous to you to understand how the return works, what types of deductions you should be tracking, and some of the choices available to you relating to your taxes and the preparation of your return.

Common Cents Saving   Vincent Brown

Before we leave the subject, I want to highlight a few other issues, some of which are mentioned elsewhere in the book but important enough to deserve re-emphasis.

Try really hard to get over the mindset that if you get a refund, life is good and if you have to write a check to the government for a dollar, everyone is out to get you. Consider two taxpayers with comparable tax situations each with a total tax liability of $5,000. One has had $8,000 withheld and will be getting a refund of $3,000, the other has had $4,500 withheld and owes $500. In the end, both taxpayers are going to end up paying the identical amount of taxes for the year. If you are the one owing $500, you have had $3,500 more in your pocket for part of the previous 12-14 months. If you thought about this in advance and planned accordingly, you have given yourself options.

It may also help to bear in mind that rather than increasing the amount of your refund, you may be better served by attempting to decrease the amount of tax you pay in total. Efforts to reduce your overall tax liability and manage your withholding will actually put more money in your pocket sooner and should make the amount of the refund much less important.

I believe that I could make myself a very rich man if I offered, and you accepted, to place a bet with me that you would be more likely to remember the approximate amount of last year's refund rather than how much your actual tax liability was. Remember, the important number is how much you actually owed for the year, not the amount you got back because you had too much paid in the first place. When I used to talk to my clients about the amount of their total tax liabilities in an effort to plan, most were shocked at how high the number was. We don't necessarily "feel" it because not only does it come out of our paychecks, but also because it is paid a little at a time.

One final point, not because it necessarily affects savings but because it is important. If you ever get the urge to assume that any notice you receive from the

IRS, especially one asking that you pay more money, is correct on its' face, please reconsider. The IRS mails out millions of computer generated notices every year and while the service is not malicious, it is also not necessarily efficient. Many, and it wouldn't be a stretch to say most, of these notices are incorrect. Never pay a balance due on a notice without some due diligence as to why it is owed. There are any number of reasons why you might owe more tax, most of them valid. But there are routinely errors in the computer generated notices that are mailed to taxpayers. All I'm saying is to use your common sense, get help if you need it but be sure that you have a feeling of reasonable assurance that the information on the notice is correct and that there aren't extenuating circumstances. Oh, and by the way, receiving a tax notice is routine and no cause for sleepless nights.

My presumption is that most of you will never be tax experts. That said, there are lots of reasons to be generally aware of your tax issues and none I can think of that would make it helpful to you to be clueless about them. Force yourself to spend some time with your return, what numbers appear on it and where, and generally where they come from. I believe you will be surprised by how much help this will be in thinking about your options and how you can save more of your hard earned money.

FIG. 2 - Personal Income Tax Return
Outline of Major Categories - Form 1040

TOTAL INCOME	XXXXX	All of your income and losses
LESS: ADJUSTMENTS TO INCOME	XXXXX	Certain deductions specifically designated by the IRS as deductible by all taxpayers from their total income
ADJUSTED GROSS INCOME	XXXXX	Total Income less the Standard or Itemized Deductions
LESS: ITEMIZED OR STAND. DEDUCTIONS	XXXXX	Total of the Standard Deduction or the total of your Itemized Deductions, whichever is greater
TAXABLE INCOME	XXXXX	Adjusted Gross Income, less Itemized or Standard Deduction. A critical number on your tax return
INCOME TAX	XXXXX	Your total income tax for the year, computed on taxable income using rates for your income and filing status
LESS: CREDITS	XXXXX	Non-refundable credits, allowed to reduce income tax dollar for dollar but only up to the total amount of income tax
PLUS: OTHER TAXES	XXXXX	Certain other non-income taxes that are required to be computed and paid on your personal tax return
TOTAL TAX	XXXXX	Your total Income Tax computed for the year less Non-Refundable Credits plus Other Taxes. This is your total liability for the year.
LESS: PAYMENTS	XXXXX	Total income taxes that have been withheld from your salaries or otherwise paid, plus refundable credits allowed
BALANCE DUE OR REFUND	XXXXX	The bottom line. The net amount of all of your taxes and the amount you will be refunded or have to pay

Banking

While perhaps not a critical element in our efforts to embrace a realistic savings program, banks do have a place in the process and it's possible that a good bank can be an ally in your plans. Banks are part of an industry which is heavily marketing driven and consider their customer data base one of their significant assets. Banks try very hard to leverage their existing relationships with customers by offering them access to an ever broadening array of service offerings. Despite their efforts and extensive marketing claims, I think the truth is that for most of us our needs are such that they can be met by almost any bank.

If it is not obvious, I believe in capitalism and don't begrudge anyone or any industry their honest efforts to make a living nor, in my opinion, should you. My judgment is that a free market, with all its flaws, will provide we consumers the opportunity to act or not act in a way that will determine which goods and services are successful, how they are provided and at what price. Having said that, I believe that for most of us folks banking is a commodity. The days of personal service and having a relationship with your banker are fading at warp speed if they are not gone altogether, especially for individual customers who do not have businesses and don't rely on their bank for loans and other business needs. When

Common Cents Saving   Vincent Brown

I had my accounting practice, I had a long time relationship with a local bank in the small community where I lived and worked. I was very comfortable with it and literally could call and get things done over the phone. They actually did me some real favors over the term of our relationship which I still appreciate. I'm, afraid that the world and the banking industry have both changed since then.

Most banks offer checking and savings accounts, monthly statements, a credit and/or debit card, and a reasonable approach to qualifying for cash free checking. Even the smallest of banks now offer on line access to your account to check balances and transfer funds between accounts. If you are serious about saving, this is important. So, how should you choose a bank? First, it may be safe to say that the larger national or regional banks are likely to be able to offer you more bells and whistles in terms of services. The question is whether you need the fringe services and are they worth the lack of flexibility that tends to be a part of how larger organizations routinely seem to operate these days. The larger the entity, the more structured the procedures are and the less authority and flexibility the local employees are likely to have. For the sake of argument, let's assume you have looked at the large/smaller bank option and made a choice. After that, for me, it boils down to a choice of convenience but here are a few additional things I suggest you think about.

First, make sure you can easily meet whatever requirements, including minimum balances, they have for cash free checking and savings. Verify that there are no significant limitations or fees to transfer money between accounts. Next, I would make sure your bank is geographically convenient to your everyday life. Some evening or Saturday morning hours might be convenient depending on your lifestyle. Confirm that they have credit and debit cards if these are a part of how you operate. Finally, understand their fee structure for everything.

I'd like to mention one service that some smaller banks may not be able to offer that I think is extremely valuable and should be a part of your household financial plan, namely on line bill pay. I expect it won't be long before every bank will have to offer it but not all do right now. Having used it for several years now, I would never choose a bank that couldn't offer it. It is efficient, economical and lends itself effectively to the mindset I am suggesting to you. Once you start using it, you will wonder why you waited so long.

Many of my friends and family are against it. I'm not sure what the real reasons are, but I am told it's because they feel more comfortable using paper checks or they think that using the on line system is dangerous and increases the risk of identity theft, fraud or other financial mishaps. They may be right, but I have to admit that I don't think so. Either way, I would find it difficult to go back to writing and mailing checks.

Generally it works like this. You go online to your account, enter who you want to pay, the amount you want to pay them and the date you want the payment to get there and forget it. That's it. And why is this a good thing, you ask? Let me see, how do I count the ways?

The service is free. You will save the postage and envelope cost of every bill you pay. For me it's one hundred to two hundred payments a year. You will save time as there is no envelope to address and seal and you don't have to remember, or take the time, to go to the Post Office or mail the envelopes. Once you enter the vendor's address one time, subsequent payments require only that you click on the vendor's name and enter an amount and the date you want the check to arrive. You can even set up recurring payments that are made as often as you like automatically. I normally enter my bills as I receive them and set a date for payment a day or two before the due date and file them away. It may take 4-5 seconds per bill. My payments do not clear my account until they are received and deposited by my vendors but you may want to check on how your bank does it. I highly recommend this to everyone who has a computer. It will make life much easier for you and will of course save you money.

Common Cents Saving   Vincent Brown

In the interest of full disclosure, if you erroneously enter $1,200.00 as payment to your utility company for a $120.00 bill, your payment will most assuredly be processed for $1,200.00. But in almost every case an error like this is easily rectified and you just have to exercise a little caution when entering amounts to be paid to individuals you don't know well, those who are just not to be trusted and perhaps the occasional relative. It goes without saying that you still have your paper checks to use for travel or when payment is required at time of service.

There is one other banking service that I suggest you consider and that is establishing a home equity line of credit on your home. You may have gathered that I am generally not a fan of debt, or more accurately unnecessary debt. There are times, however when funds are needed in the short term, perhaps even for the purchase of an automobile. Interest on auto loans, other installment loans and credit card interest are not deductible for tax purposes. Only interest secured by your home is deductible if you itemize your deductions (and now you know exactly what I am talking about). Having a home equity line in place gives you instant access to funds when needed, the interest on which can be fully tax deductible. It also may provide a lower interest rate and more flexible payments than most installment loans. When I got mine, there was no cost at all associated with qualifying as the bank was happy to provide the line at no cost to me. I am not sure if that is still the case, or how many hoops you may have to jump through to qualify in the current climate, but if you do have equity in your home, consider setting it up. A lot has changed in banking but the old adage is still true. The best time to apply for and qualify for a loan is before you need one.

The overall message is that most banks tend to look alike and selecting one should be based more on practicalities than glitz. Avoid service charges and check fees, see if their location and hours are convenient for you and select a bank that allows for on line bill pay to save postage and handling and you will be ahead of the game. It occurs to me that thus far I have not stated the obvious but I will do so now. Please do use a bank for the majority of your money. Your mattress, a box buried in the yard or the coffee can in the cabinet are less than stable alternatives.

I can't resist one final admonition. Let me start by saying that I understand that we are not all perfect or as organized as we would like. In addition, things occasionally happen beyond our control and we are bound to just slip up on occasion. Nonetheless, if you routinely incur overdraft charges, stop payment fees and other bank charges through our own lack of attention or carelessness, you are simply not taking care of business. I have been blown away over the years by the amount of unnecessary annual bank charges that some people incur. If you are serious about saving and about retaining your hard-earned funds for your future, you simply have to work at avoiding excessive charges like these that provide no incremental value to you and could have been avoided with a little more care.

And finally, reconcile your checking account and review your credit card statement on a monthly basis. It doesn't take that long to reconcile your account, the more you do it the better you will get it and the easier it will become. You might also be aware that most computer accounting programs have a bank reconciliation feature which may be another incentive to consider one. As to your credit card statement, you may not want to match up every receipt to the statement like I do but you should be totally familiar with every charge on it. You can't own your own financial well-being if you don't invest your own time in managing it.

In summary, while your banking relationship may not be critical to you, at a minimum we should all use a bank and have a checking account, so try and make your choice as to where to place your business so that it works for you.

Common Cents Saving   **Vincent Brown**

Kids and Family - You Gotta Love 'Em

There aren't many things in our life that produce more exquisite highs or gut wrenching lows than family. Because of the powerful financial and emotional impact that our families have on us, I believe the subject deserves separate consideration as to its' potential impact on our savings goals. Admittedly, attempting to separate the financial issues relating to our families from the emotional and interpersonal considerations is a lofty goal but a reality and one certainly worthy of our efforts. More to the point, it is an effort that is key to your success in maintaining a savings bias. I am not saying that we can effectively isolate our family's financial and interpersonal issues. I do offer, however, that the continued awareness that they exist and may put us in conflict, requires that you attempt to manage them on your journey. Further complicating things for us is that both the family financial and interpersonal issues are different for all of us and significantly influenced by the various needs, expectations and personalities of each member of the family and other interested parties. I seldom had planning discussions with any of my clients where their prevailing family dynamics did not materially influence our discussions and objectives often in very unique ways.

By way of background, I grew up in a family of modest means with a mother and father, myself and three younger sisters. We had a home, beds to sleep in (some in the same room) and, thanks to my Italian mom, great food to eat but not a lot more. Vacations were occasional if not rare; we never ate out though every few months we might bring in subs or pizza; we might load up for the drive-in once a summer but that was about it; no movies, baseball games or other entertainment until we were able to save for it ourselves. We were always proximate to my seven sets of aunts and uncles on my Italian mother's side and their children, my 50 or so cousins so that the family was close and that provided for a lot of our activities.

I've been through my share of therapy and read a sufficient number of self-help books that I have had occasion to consider my life in terms of what I had too much of and what may have been lacking. I have put in the requisite time and effort pondering what, if anything I should consider hating my parents for. My conclusion was, is and always will be that whatever could be said about my parents, my childhood, my wife, my children and other family members, it is perfectly clear to me that what I have or don't have, what I am or am not, at this point in my life is one hundred percent the result of my past choices and my determination and dexterity at reacting to those choices.

My expectation is that you will always be intimately involved with your family in a healthy way but whether you are or not, they should never be the cause of, or take the blame for, you not taking care of yourself. I believe this should be true for every adult in our society.

Our family now consists of me and my wife of 45 years, three grown children all of whom live or have lived nearby here in Maine with all but one of our eight grandchildren. In addition I feel blessed to have what I believe is a terrific relationship with my three sisters and their husbands as well as my wife's brother's family. The dynamics of every family is different but in the spectrum of relative levels of family chaos, I offer the perspective that my situation was and is, if not normal, then certainly not extreme. Everyone may not agree with that assessment but my objective here is to give you my perspective.

Over the course of a lifetime, we look to and from family members for substantially different things at different times. Varying perceptions, expectations and needs will certainly evolve differently in each family unit. It is an understatement to say that these impressions and expectations are unpredictable. As a trite example, over the years, any discussions with my sisters about what it was like in my home growing up would force any sane person to conclude that none of us lived in the same home, with the same people under the same circumstances. For whatever reason, it would seem clear that our house reflected some twilight zone of alternating realties which materialized depending on which of us was looking. This one example of diverse interpretation of seemingly identical experiences alone makes it easy for me to see how we might develop differing views on our responsibilities to our parents, them to us and us to each other.

The simple fact is that there can be no doubt that immediate and extended family issues can pose challenges to you and the financial plans I have encouraged you to make a part of your life. We are likely all familiar with families where the needs just never end. In other words, it's the polar opposite of the gifts that keep on giving. When it comes to the family and the need to face tough financial decisions on issues relating to them, allow me to offer some encouragement wrapped in what I hope is common sense. I would like you to remember that you are not alone, there are things you can do to at least help structure those decisions and most importantly, there may be times when you can, should or must say no.

I am aware of the possible violations to political correctness that we are flirting with here should we try to apply analytics to any of the emotional, financial or other needs of our family. That said, bear with me and see where this goes. The consideration of kids and family can literally be a runaway train. I have seen it with my clients and friends and my guess is that you have also. I suggest it will be easier for us to deal with these very emotional issues if we are able to create a little structure in which to do so which includes, however slightly or remotely, the notion of objectivity as part of the process. This may be something much easier said than done but is essential to us if we are to try to stay on course with our bias to save.

For starters, let's discuss family in three separate categories, namely our children, our grandchildren and others to include brothers, sisters-in-law, cousins, nieces, nephews and well you get it. I've taken the liberty of excluding any discussion of your parents assuming that you are reasonably adult and their influence or dependence on you, financially and otherwise, is minimal at this point in your life. In the event that this is not the case, the following still applies but you will have additional obstacles to overcome. As I indicated earlier, we must also assume that you and your spouse or significant other, if you have one, have gone through whatever process was necessary to come to substantial unanimity as to the guidelines and goals to be employed when confronted with issues relating to family obligations, financial and otherwise. Yes, I know that is quite the stipulation but I think we can all agree, a necessary one.

I believe that we can agree that each of us has a different financial reality and consequently a different ability to help. In addition, we are all over the lot in terms of what our perception is of our responsibilities to our families, some realistic and some pretty out there. To top it off, we have diverse families with a myriad of financial, physical and emotional needs. Perhaps the only common denominator in these conflicting circumstances is that most of us instinctively want to, and believe that we should, help and it is flat out really hard to say "no".

Let's deal with "other family" first where I believe it is easiest to be objective and reign in emotions. I'm not sure what it says about me, but I was generally lacking a compelling commitment to assume a role in the financial struggles of my siblings, in-laws, cousins, and their families. Hopefully I had the ability to be sympathetic, but I have no built in predisposition to help these relatives financially. In fact, I would have to acknowledge that only if I were presented a fairly unique set of circumstances, would I have helped out in a meaningful financial way. You have to admit that an open ended commitment to financially help extended family and all that entails is both a daunting and unrealistic goal. We are all free to make exceptions for extenuating circumstances of course but my reluctance (shared with my spouse) was a yardstick for me. It encouraged me to remain focused on my plans for my immediate family and my savings goals based on my personal values and priorities.

> **Potential Future Financial Needs For Our Children**
>
> •*Private School*
> •*Camps*
> •*Developing A Unique Gift*
> •*Cell Phone*
> •*Car*
> •*College*
> •*Wedding*
>
> *Private school averages $10,000 to $17,000 per year. The average annual college cost is $23,000 for public in state schools and $44,000 for private school. A generic, non-specialty camp averages $3,500 per month. The average wedding costs $26,000. Overall, the current estimated cost to raise a child through college is $286,000 to $317,000.*

As to our kids, the emotional and financial complexities compound exponentially. My first suggestion for you is to think and talk about the obvious, and perhaps not so obvious, types of financial needs you might anticipate for your children down the road before you have to face them. The list to the left of this page is a sampling of these. When you have a fairly generic list together it will likely be helpful to look at the options, talk about them as realistically as possible and toss around a few initial guidelines.

Objectively, what help do you think is most important given limited resources? How much help is enough? There is nothing that contributes more to the solution of a complex problem than a frame of reference that you have vetted beforehand. You may have to change it or scrap it but you may be surprised how far it will take you if it has been thought out properly. So, as specifically as you can at whatever point in life you find yourself, set out your plans for your children's needs. Next, whatever you do, communicate your plans to your children right away and remind them of them often. Let them know if they have to change. The more seriously you take them, the more likely that your children will naturally accept them as a reality they have to deal with.

Take college for instance. We felt a desire and responsibility to provide a lot of encouragement and some assistance for college but knew we could not provide all of the costs for the three of them. We established a plan early on that was communicated often and in detail to our children. At some point when the kids were in grade school we put a modest deposit in a college fund for each of our children. Annually thereafter, assuming it was feasible, we set aside a much smaller, but predetermined annual amount for each of them in their account. This amount was obviously a part of our annual budgeted expenditures Our intent, which they knew, was that whatever funds were in their account when they went off to school would be applied to their college costs. In addition, we would try to help with living expenses while at school. The cost of school in excess of the amount we had saved for them would have to be funded by them, through loans or other means for which they would have to assume responsibility for payment. I believe that over the years we ended up saving approximately the equivalent of a year to a year and a half of their college costs. They borrowed the rest and subsequently paid the loans off through their own effort. This was our approach. The important thing to us in retrospect was that we thought about it in advance, did what we thought we could do on a consistent basis, communicated it all to the kids and most importantly, heeded the words of Dr. Samuel Johnson "Nothing will ever be attempted, if all possible objections must be first overcome"[5]. To us this meant we did not want to fall into the trap of doing nothing because we couldn't do it all.

As to your children's other potential needs when they get married, separated, divorced, back together, change jobs, move, want to buy homes, cars or run into other hardships, we dealt with each of these issues as they arose but did so in the context of our overall goals and current situation. Again, in the interest of

---

5 John Shanahan, *The Most Brilliant Thoughts of All Time*, Harper Collins Publishers, 1999, p. 155

full disclosure, we made them all aware that we expected them to take care of themselves. As those of you who have families know, things come up. One of our guiding considerations was to make sure we were fair to all three by committing ourselves to treating them equally financially. Of course, in the real world this is a difficult thing to do. When it wasn't possible to assist them equally, we made it clear what was a gift and what was a loan and also tracked amounts advanced to one but not the others. Our stipulation to them was that any differential in these gifts or unpaid loans would be settled up from our estate, if there was one, prior to distributing the remainder in equal shares to them. This provision is included in our will as well as instructions as to where to find the calculations of the remaining balances owed by each.

None of us are immune from second guessing. I think it's fair to say that we may have helped slightly less than we might have but certainly more than we expected. I don't need to emphasize how difficult these evaluations can be and why. Often the needs of our children arise through circumstances beyond their control and occasionally beyond their capacity to address effectively. Of course, there is also the reality that some of their needs may be directly related to their neglect or recklessness. The critical thing here is that a general approach to how you hope to make these judgments should be openly discussed and hashed out between the spouses early on and hopefully communicated to your children. But make no mistake, they are a significant factor in your financial security. My best advice to you is to set up some general guidelines for yourselves and make the children aware of them before you are faced with the situation. It will give you some perspective, encourage you to think about the matter objectively before you are knee deep into a highly charged emotional situation and may help avoid or minimize unrealistic expectations in the children. That said, you and I both know that no matter how much we discuss and settle on an approach before the fact, the emotional stress on us from real life charging at us fast and hard will always make these decisions horribly difficult. My best advice is to try to bring what little objectivity you can to the problem, make the best decision you can based on your predefined objectives and current ability to help and don't beat yourself up about it afterward. And of course don't forget the obvious, namely that while it will be difficult, a response of "no" is one of your options. I'm sure you've noticed that having "no" as an option is pretty important in much of what we are discussing here.

Now, as to grandchildren, that is another story entirely isn't it? If you are grandparents you know exactly what I mean. If you are not, I hope you are lucky enough to be someday. We have all seen grandparents who are all over the lot with their grandchildren and who am I to attempt to assess how much is too much? I will first say that you should enjoy your grandchildren. They are, to my mind, one of life's pleasant little surprises that, if you are fortunate, show up in your life just when we are at an age when you could use a lift. For what it's worth, my personal opinion (and hardly objective) is that grandparents should be free to spoil their grandchildren at any time at any place within reason but without overriding their parent's wishes. Having said that, I believe that significant purchases or support may send the wrong message and perhaps inhibit the grandchild's journey to take charge of their life and make his/her own way. Needless to say, my kids believe that whatever I do or don't do, I am overwhelmingly more indulgent in all ways with their children than I was with them. They are probably right. After all, I am a different person in a different place in my life. Hopefully, I have learned a few things along the way. Interestingly though, I have to say that I feel comfortable that I am keeping my eye on the ball when it comes to holding to the basic financial goals, however modified, that we set a long time ago and also in trying to support and encourage the values in my grandchildren that I hold important and tried to teach my children. Equally important, my children understand and get it.

Other than the routine Christmas and birthday gifts and the occasional movie, lunch or trip for ice cream with them, our only direct financial commitment to the grandchildren is a modest amount set aside in their account at each of their birthdays until they turn 18. Each has an account set up under the "Uniform Gift to Minors Act" in their Social Security numbers with their names and mine on the account. To the best of my knowledge they and their parents do not know the accounts are there. On the other hand, a family is like a small town on steroids and it is hard to keep too many secrets. These individual accounts will not amount to enough to significantly alter their lives but may be helpful to them in getting a car or going to school. Besides it sure has made us feel good about being able to do it for them.

You may think it is contrary to your concept of family to approach your children's crises in any way analytically. No doubt it is in many ways and I doubt we can ever approach decisions about our children totally clinically. I do think, however, that all financial decisions should be somewhat grounded in reality and put to some degree of analysis and scrutiny. We are lucky. Our kids are wonderful, independent people. They assume responsibility for themselves and their actions, of course more so now than they may have as teenagers. We would love to do all we can for them but like you, we can only do what we are able and willing to do. They understand and accept this. One of the things we may have done well is having communicated with them consistently about our financial situation and plans for them, including after we are gone.

My objective with this book remains to encourage you to commit yourselves during your working life to a plan of savings that balances a full and rich life while planning for a secure financial future and options at retirement. Without question, this is a lofty goal. I expect that your plan will include a balance of your best effort to do all that you can for your children and other family members as you are saving for this sound financial future. Nothing worth anything is easy and this certainly won't be but it can be done. More to the point, we both know that the real issue is that it has to be done.

I'd like to make one final and perhaps unrelated comment. I can't tell you how many times in my career I have seen families do irreparable harm to themselves after one or more of the parents dies and the estate is being distributed, often in cases when the amount of money involved is not even significant. I really don't know what to say about this that will be meaningful to you but I will try anyway. Parents, make your kids at least generally aware of the provisions of your will, who is the executor of your estate, what your financial intentions are and what your expectations of them are after you go. For you survivors, other than advise you to be decent and honorable human beings and caution you that a little money will never end up being more important than your remaining family, you're on your own. Referring back to the "making it a game" approach, if you don't think about the fact that you may inherit something, or how much it could be, then anything you get will be welcomed and gratefully received. Other than that, it sort of still boils down to trying to be decent and honorable people.

There is a final word of caution to those of you who elect to take on the responsibility of caring for your infirmed family members while they are alive. If you harbor any expectations that you are to be compensated for your efforts from their estate when they pass on, document this fact, in writing, at the outset including the amount you are to be paid. Obviously, the person you are caring for needs to be of sound mind and in agreement and will acknowledge this by signing to the terms. If you value your siblings and your relationship with them, I strongly advise that they know what those arrangements are also. Settle the details before the fact. Without a legally binding agreement to pay you, there is very likely no legal remedy for you to be paid for these efforts from the estate after the fact, the presumption being that you performed the services voluntarily as family member to family member. I'm not saying the other siblings or heirs couldn't agree to pay you without an agreement, just that they are under no obligation to do so and, based on my experience, very likely won't. Disputes like this routinely result in hard feelings, destroyed relationships with siblings and a mess. If you are not caring for your parents or other relative solely because you choose to do so and think it's the right thing, don't do it or arrange for some scheduled compensation in advance that everyone else in the family is aware of (whether or not they like it).

Retirement Plans

The most meaningful thing I can say about retirement plans is that they are invaluable if you are serious about saving. A major premise of this work is that one of the motivations for saving is an expansion of choices relating to retirement. Much of what we have talked about up to this point relates to techniques for what to do with after tax dollars, in other words your take home pay. This was especially important to me as a self-employed person for most of my working life. I only once worked for an employer who had a retirement plan and that plan did not provide for employer contributions. I maximized my voluntary contributions to the plan, realized the tax deferral on my contributions but the benefit of having someone else's money put aside for me was not available. For those of you fortunate enough to work for an employer who offers a retirement plan or plans, especially if your employer contributes or matches contributions, you are a leg up on many of us so please, do what you can to take advantage of it. Unfortunately, the trend is that fewer and fewer private employers are willing to offer retirement plans, and even fewer offer employer contributions or matching features. As you might expect, the large majority of governmental employees are still very well served by liberal plans, most with employer contributions which some (myself included) might say are lavish in light of the fact that we, the public, are paying for them.

In the current environment of financial instability in our country qualified retirement plans, if available to you and for as long as they last, should be a cornerstone of your planning process. While I am generally cynical about the security of a lot of things these days, retirement plans may be among the most secure of many of our options. It's hard to overemphasize just how important they can be as a part of your financial plan before you even think about saving part of your take home pay.

You should also consider that the traditional concept of retirement may be redefining itself as a result of recent events. There are millions of work age Americans who have vacated the work force before they wanted to, the long-term status of Medicare may be in question, the future of the Social Security system is sketchy and certainly requires some restructuring, the national debt is at critical levels and there are historically high numbers of people on government subsidy programs with efforts underway to even increase those numbers exponentially. The conventional model of thirty five years of service with one or more companies and retiring comfortably with a secure pension may be going the way of the drive-in movie (unless you live in Maine where we still seem to have drive-in movie theaters). If people my age have already had to rethink their retirement plans it stands to reason that you younger folks may be facing even more question marks when the time comes for you.

There is no way of telling if any of this will change or even if there is a will or consensus that it should. Regardless of whether you are of a mind that it is government's role to see that we are cared for or not , keep in mind that as the needs of citizens increase the government is likely to be stretched beyond its' capability of addressing these needs. It seems to me that if you hope to be able to retire as comfortably as possible and not just scrape by, it's not a bad idea to accept your share of the responsibility for making it happen for you which is yet another compelling reason to save. As to whether we, as a country, will continue to allow us to do this is, of course, another question.

An essential point about retirement plans is that funding them should be part of your day to day living expenses whenever possible; in other words, part of what you budget to spend before you have a surplus to save. Funding savings is not a substitute for funding your retirement plan but rather an addition to it.

When I use the term "retirement plan" I mean structured plans provided by your employer or those available to you personally to set up and administer yourself like 401K and IRA plans. They are sometimes referred to as "qualified plans". These plans are totally different from and superior to what we have generically been referring to as savings for a number of reasons. First, qualified retirement plans have the advantage of generating Federal and State tax savings on the contributions made to them. Second, all earnings and gains generated within the plans are not currently taxable as they are incurred. Finally, some employers contribute (match) some or all of your contributions) which is hitting the grand slam in savings parlance as *it is not your money* that is being saved for you. I am afraid that the number of employers making or matching contributions for employees may be dwindling in today's economic climate (with the exception of the government of course) but there are still some. The insert in this chapter provides a few statistics regarding who has retirement plans. It is significant to note that plans in private industry, if they exist, may be non-contributory and are fading fast. While the overall number of Americans covered by plans has decreased only about

---

Who Has Retirement Plans?

William J. Wiatrowski, in an essay in the December 2012 Monthly Labor Review, indicates that in 2011, only 10% of all private sector establishments provided retirement plans, and this percentage is declining annually. Despite this, retirement plans are still prevalent among government workers as most federal government employees and 78% of state and local employees have plans.

Considering all employees in the workplace, those covered by an employer-sponsored pension plan went from about 40% in 1990 to less than 20% in 2011.

20% in the last 21 years, this decrease is much higher in the private sector due to the increase in Federal, State and local government employees (virtually all of which are covered) in a generally decreasing overall workforce. Putting aside the big government, little government debate, the reality for all of us is that funding those government pension obligations has to be borne by taxes paid by non-government employed Americans who are not likely to be covered themselves. If you are one of those, recognizing that you are funding public sector benefits and retirement at increasing levels, it only makes sense to take steps to try and do whatever you can for yourself. Believe me, no one else will.

The fact that there are penalties for withdrawing the funds from our qualified plans early may be an advantage or disadvantage depending on your particular situation, how disciplined you are or even how you look at it. Simply put, because it will cost us financially to access money from these plans before we're supposed to, this may be all the incentive we need to leave them alone and a clear advantage over easy access to savings with no current tax or penalty cost. On the other hand, if you should need this money prematurely, then the tax and penalty cost of withdrawing retirement funds early would be a deterrent to contributing to these plans as opposed to merely saving the money. We both hope that this doesn't happen but our expectation up front should be that all contributions to qualified retirement plans will be left intact to compound over the years on a tax deferred basis until we can withdraw them without penalty.

Here is my specific advice about retirement plans and funding them. Without putting your family at risk, and within the parameters of your own good judgment, do all that you can to maximize the amount that you contribute, and the amount eligible to be contributed by others on your behalf, to qualified retirement plans. If you can't maximize contributions, put the emphasis on making as much of a contribution as you can to take advantage of your employer's matching provisions. In addition to your employer's retirement plans, if you can do so, make individual IRA or 401K deductions at least to the dollar amount where they are deductible on your tax returns but higher if you can. This may seem an obvious thing to do but I assure you it is not obvious for everyone.

Your commitment to these qualified plans is routinely the best, most advantageous way to build a base for a plan of retirement security. Assuming you have what you think is a reasonable reserve of cash to see you through emergencies, consider allocating the major portion of any current surplus earnings over expenses to qualified plan contributions and the rest to savings. It goes without saying that you should do whatever you have to do to create a mindset that those retirement contributions are to be left alone. If I haven't said it, my presumption is that your savings funds will serve, in part, as the vehicle to access in the case of emergencies and not your retirement accounts.

As always, it needs to be said that no one size fits all. It makes no sense to commit funds to retirement plan that you know you will need. It makes even less sense, however, to not make contributions that you can afford. Get some outside advice if you need it but your retirement plan is one of the biggest opportunities you have to help yourself out down the road. Do all that you can within the limitations of your financial reality to make it work for you.

For some of you, your pension and Social Security benefits may be sufficient for you to have a satisfying and stress free (at least financially) retirement. This may be the case for a large percentage of public sector employees. I don't offer this as a criticism or complaint (at least in this context) but as my assessment of what is real. Whatever your current situation, even if you are one of the fortunate ones, if you are many years from retirement, consider that there is no guarantee that you will keep your job or that your employer will keep its' qualified plan. Further, there is no way to tell what life is going to throw at you or what the world will look like when you retire. In short, it's important for all of us to take advantage of our retirement plans while we can and save in addition to give yourself the best opportunities for the best outcomes.

Vacations, Toys and Other Goodies

This chapter is short but certainly not because the topics are not critical elements of your plans to save. It might be fair to say that, other than family, the types of expenditures discussed in this chapter may be some of the biggest obstacles you will face in trying to achieve your goals. The reason the chapter is short is simply because there is only so much that can be said about those tough personal choices that only you can make. These choices include those special activities in our life that give us a lift, spice things up and manage to keep us going when things get tough. They are also, without question, temptations that in many cases must be successfully dealt with. They are never far from view, always attractive and the subject of billions of dollars of relentless and seductive advertising. I'm referring to vacations, entertainment, gifts, grown-up toys and the occasional splurge or impulse buy.

The first point that needs to be made is to make sure that your monthly estimate for living expenses contains a reasonable allowance for all of these things. If it doesn't the amount you have committed to save will not be realistic, you will have grave difficulty in sticking to your plan and you are likely to be frustrated and resentful throughout the process. Remember, the general idea includes an attempt to act like a grown up even though we would rather do a lot of stuff that grown-ups tend not to do.

Having made it clear that your plan should include allowances for those fun things in your life, it unfortunately now becomes necessary to examine the fine print. I'm guessing that you had to know this was coming. Despite our efforts to plan for what I am referring to as "goodies", for many of us, especially if you are working on a tight budget, you can count on their being more opportunities to spend on goodies than we have provided for. In addition, while we are likely to underestimate the cost of our play activities when planning, human nature will encourage us to emotionally overvalue them when we are faced with the decision to finance them. This is the struggle that faces all of us.

Family and fun are the two areas that we need to wrestle with most when it comes to the battle over what is best for our future and what is emotionally expedient now. I have no answers of course, just some observations and encouragement. These choices are part of everyday life and can be managed effectively and with less pain if we take a breath and keep our wits about us. Simply put, making significant financial decisions based solely on how we feel at the moment is a hazard to your financial health. The first thing I suggest you do is to be realistic when planning these expenses for the year which means, at a minimum, don't kid yourself. By definition, they are goodies, they are everywhere, they make us feel good and only the dullest and most boring of us are immune to their charm.

Next, look long and hard when facing those inevitable additional choices that you did not include in your plans for the year. Attempt to minimize the hazard by committing yourself to a little internal soul searching and ask yourself a few questions prior to taking the plunge. Why didn't you budget for it? Why does it seem so important today when it wasn't then? Is it important enough to warrant the future financial impact on your life? At least slow the process down. This may not seem like such a big deal but it is more than a lot of us do and will at least give you some time to reflect. There is little downside to taking a second look, the choice is still yours and even if you end up doing what you wanted to do in the first place, you have applied some judgment to the process.

Included in my former clients were some champion savers. Some saved effectively and had what it took to do so happily without adversely interfering with their life. They kept things in perspective and were able to adjust to life as it happened. They weren't afraid to face tough decisions and didn't second guess themselves. Mostly, they were reasonable and trusted their ability to manage priorities and my impression was that the very process infused them with a sense of contentment and accomplishment. In other words, they allowed themselves to think outside the box but felt that they were in control of the choices involved in the process.

On the other hand, some of my good saver clients were not so effective and, in my view, lacked perspective. Terms like neurotic, bizarre and miserable come to mind. If you recall Dustin Hoffman in the movie "Rain Man", picture these people repeating over and over "I am an excellent saver". Whether they were on the lower or higher end of the financial ladder, they achieved satisfactory results but couldn't manage the process effectively. They might spend days off cruising local towns to interview banks in search of a CD that paid a quarter of a point higher rate. To be fair, that was back in the day when you could actually get a decent rate on a CD but you get my point. They looked like they hadn't bought clothes since adolescence. One couple actually told me they couldn't understand why people would spend money to travel if it meant paying to sleep somewhere else when they had a perfectly good bed at home. Whatever their financial status (and often it was substantial) they apparently never felt it was enough. It was of course, not only enough but often over the top excessive. Despite my recurring admonitions, they were never able (or willing) to stop, look around and enjoy what they had. As for the chicken and the egg question, could be they were doomed to be miserable anyway and they were just coincidentally savers (this would be my guess) or possibly being savers made them miserable. Either way, there is a lesson

Common Cents Saving   Vincent Brown

to be learned as evidenced by an old American proverb which claims "It is an easy matter for a stingy man to get rich-but what's the use?"

As some ammunition for you while you are in the midst of living your life and struggling with the discipline of saving now for some benefit later, let me offer some first-hand experience on why it is a good thing to do. When you do find yourself at a place in your life where you are dealing with retirement, slowing down or just getting older believe me when I say that your perspective changes significantly. You will likely be looking for a richer life including freedom, flexibility and new experiences. You will think more seriously about how you spend your time, where exactly you want to live and how you want to be remembered. If you don't have a bucket list already, I believe you will create one at this time in your life. If you have one, it will get longer. Be realistic about where you would like to put yourself financially to be able to decide about these things. I am not imparting any cosmic wisdom by assuring you that it will be here sooner than you think. Think about it as often as you can. I believe it was Yogi Berra who said something akin to "If you don't know where you're going, you may not get there". When you do arrive at that "retirement" stage, if you have made no plans and are limited financially, it's not the end of the world and you will survive but it will impact negatively on your life. Oscar Wilde said, "No man is rich enough to buy back his past"[6].

Since it is the entire point of this book, I am only slightly concerned with beating my point to death. I am hoping to encourage you to take a course of action in your life that gives you more choices as you get on in years. I don't know what choices you will want to make then but I do know that it matters that you have the option to make them. For me, I was faced with such a choice. I reached a point of conflict in my last job which was a very good one, both challenging and financially lucrative. My age at the time, fifty-five, and a dicey economy led me to believe that a lateral move or anything like it did not appear to be an option. I was faced with

---

6 John Shanahan, *The Most Brilliant Thoughts of All Time*, Harper Collins Publishers, 1999, p. 26

the decision to retire ten years earlier than I had planned or try and stick it out. My efforts over the years made it possible for me to consider such a choice. It was by no means a sure thing, but the point is, I had the option of giving it a shot. I took the risk, left the job and those ten extra retirement years have been everything I could have hoped them to be. Not to mention the fact that I removed the conflict associated with the job from my life and was able to write this book.

In summary, be realistic about all of the opportunities you deal with to have fun in your life. You need some of them, they are valuable to you and a part of a happy, successful life. At the same time, there is a cost to all of them, so put on your big person pants and understand that no one can have it all. It is not unfair to say that many of us are less than successful at making these tough calls and electing the elusive "no" word. Perhaps it is even unfair that the better off you are financially, the easier it may be to do. Either way, you are the only one in your situation and the only one who can manage it for yourself. All I am suggesting is that you bring some reason, structure and discipline to the situation. If you do, you will be glad you did.

Common Cents Saving **Vincent Brown**

Homes and Cars: Life's Major Purchases

Without doubt, for most of us, the purchase of a home or a car represents some of the major financial choices we make in life and consequently most of you are at least generally familiar with the ins and outs of these transactions. On the other hand, the fact that they are so significant and impactful to our financial status leads me to want to address them if only in a cursory way. The decision to purchase a car or real estate is similar in that they are both significant financial commitments requiring a big chunk of our available day-to-day cash, but at the same time they are significantly different in many other ways so let's talk about them.

The financial implications attendant to the purchase of a home or other real estate has changed drastically in just the last ten plus years. Whether we are talking about your personal residence or investment property, caution is the word of the day here. For those of you fortunate enough to have cash available for a real estate purchase for investment, my sense is that you have less to worry about than those who are looking to commit to their first home or a new home. A shaky economy, the downturn in the real estate market and job insecurity has made what used to be a no brainer decision now much less so. For most of my working life, despite a market with much higher interest rates, I was advising my clients to do everything they could to get themselves into their own home and to buy investment real estate, if they were able, as a part of their efforts at saving. Not only did I push them to buy, I encouraged them not to worry about initially overextending themselves by considering a purchase for slightly more than they could immediately afford with the expectation they would grow and prosper into a financial comfort zone with their payments.

I believe this advice was financially sound at the time and people prospered from it. The lack of any tax or financial benefit to renting, the deductibility of the mortgage interest, the expectation of the property appreciating, special tax considerations on the profit at sale, not to mention the non-financial perk of pride of ownership made a home purchase priority one in the financial picture. Those whose circumstances allowed it often purchased second homes, rental properties, land and time shares in addition to their residences hoping to take advantage of the "can't lose" real estate environment. At the risk of over generalizing, as long as you could manage the down payment and carrying costs, this strategy was a sound one.

As you know, circumstances have changed. Almost inconceivably, with interest rates and corresponding monthly mortgage payments as low as they are, not only is the purchase of a home no longer a slam dunk decision, it may not even be a sound one. To utilize the biggest little word ever, namely "if", if you are in good financial condition, and if you are sure you are paying close to the real market price, and if you are confident that you can and will own the property for a reasonably extended period of time, it may be a terrific time to buy, especially for investment property. Prices are low, interest rates are low, you have an unusually large inventory of homes to choose from and some sellers are, unfortunately, desperate.

On the other hand, I can think of any number of scenarios where the purchase of real estate in our present economy may be too risky to consider. Yes, I know in the case of your own residence everyone has to live somewhere and paying rent is wasted money and you get no tax benefit for it and on and on. And yes, low interest rates can mean your monthly rent may be similar to, or even more than, what the mortgage payment would be on the same house. But it is also true that people are losing their jobs in record numbers, home values have declined significantly and annual appreciation on your property is far from guaranteed. In addition, if you already own a home and have to sell it in order to buy another one, unless you have sufficient equity in your current place, the decrease in market value and sluggish market may make selling it problematic. Only you can assess your personal job security, financial situation and risk tolerance. There is no shortage of homeowners out there who are dying to move but circumstances won't allow it or will cause them to do so at their own financial risk. There are others who are making monthly payments on mortgages where the loan balance is significantly higher than the house is worth in today's market.

Do I have any sage advice if you are looking to buy? No more than the obvious I'm afraid. I never thought I would say this but renting isn't the end of the world. Depending on your circumstances, amidst so much uncertainty I think that I would have to feel pretty confident that I would be able to stay in the home at least five to ten years before I would jump into it.

There are indications that the real estate market may be picking up a bit and that the decline in real estate values may have bottomed out but, make no mistake, we are a long way from the good old days. Be realistic about your financial situation and how much of a savings cushion you have. Be very attentive to what the market is like in your locale because there is a big difference in the markets and values depending on where you are geographically. I will say this. We have a tendency to want what we want. More than once I have been accused of introducing gloom and doom into the process of making a purchase decision like this one. That doesn't change the fact that uncertainty is rampant everywhere. The potential need for a short term turn around on a recently purchased home is inherently problematic. If job loss, illness or other circumstances dictate the possibility of having to move, sell or both too soon after purchase of the property not only do you have no guarantees, but you have reason for legitimate concern. Of course, this is especially true if you have little cushion with which to absorb a loss on your home if you are forced to sell.

There is no formula you can apply here. Every set of circumstances is unique and all of the elements of those circumstances may be critical to the decision making process. There is little I can tell you that you probably don't already know except to be cautious. Consider that a tolerable outcome on a future sale will likely necessitate your holding the place for a reasonable number of years and that if forced into a quick sale, it may be messy. You might also consider that the more committed you are to your selling price, and certainly if it is unrealistic, the longer you are likely to sit on your home before it sells. My three children have purchased homes during the last ten years, all of which are still owned. I doubt that any of them could be sold for what they have invested in them. Personally, my wife and I have made the decision to down size. Our home in Maine is listed for sale. We have owned it for eleven years and will consider ourselves lucky if we can limit our loss to ten percent of our investment.

> ### A Few Housing Stats
> - *In 2006, the average price of a home for sale in the United States was $255,000. In 2012, it was $175,000.*
> - *Studies done for 2012 indicate that, all costs considered, you are financially better off renting your home if you stay there five years or less. Only after five years are the cumulative costs of buying less than renting.*
> - *Most experts believe that in 2012 volatility in housing prices is most influenced by the geographic location of the home and the strength of the school system.*

While we are talking about homes, let's take a look at the question of whether to pay off your mortgage if you are one of those fortunate folks financially liquid enough to do so. It is one of the questions I have been most asked over the years. Despite the fact that many of us may never have this opportunity and if we do, it will be very late in our life, I still think it is a subject worth discussing if for no other reason than to consider the dynamics involved in this type of decision. This is another classic choice more influenced by non-financial considerations than science. The choice is do you reduce your savings and potentially limit your liquidity to eliminate your monthly mortgage payment and avoid all that interest you would have paid over the mortgage term. I will purposely exclude the income tax considerations of the decision, not because it is not an issue, but more to simplify things and because for many of us especially those in lower tax brackets it may be less an issue than it has been in the past.

Here is the meat of it for me. If you were able to assure me that if you paid off your mortgage today, every month thereafter the amount that was your mortgage payment would be faithfully put into your savings (essentially paid to yourself), all other things being equal, it's an easy decision for me. By all means, take your savings and pay off your mortgage. Remember, I said, all things being equal but as we know, life is seldom that way.

When I have had this conversation with clients over the years and have asked for the commitment to replace the mortgage payment with a check to replenish savings, I was surprised at how few people could, or would, commit. Making a mortgage payment has been termed a method of forced savings. This is especially relevant with mortgage rates as low as they now are. So, I will advise you as I advised my clients over the years. If you are not reasonably sure that you can divert what was your mortgage payment back into savings on a reasonably consistent basis, then consider keeping your mortgage in place. This keeps what you have saved intact and forces you to continue your monthly payment from current funds that you acknowledge might not be saved otherwise. The truth is that this is a decision that needs to be made based on where you are in life, your individual personality traits and what your goals and expectations are.

To wrap up our discussion on the purchase of real estate considering the economics in place halfway through 2013, the important thing to remember is that no one size fits all. If you are considering the purchase of a home as your primary residence and your resources are limited, while the prices and interest rates are right, the short term implications pose a significant risk if you are forced to sell. In the case of investment property, if you are financially able to do so and you believe, as many are telling us, that this is the bottom and an upswing is expected, you can be much more optimistic but no less cautious. Don't strap yourself, make sure you are buying at the market and do your homework.

As to cars, if this chapter were about how much I know about them, this would be the last sentence in it. For most of us, the need for a car is unavoidable and a significant recurring expense in our lives. Assuming that the possibility exists that we may occasionally overspend in this area, and I do assume this, there may be some value in talking about how we approach that need and how it relates to our savings goals. As far as I'm concerned, it is possible that the conflict between our emotions and reality may rear its ugly head more often at the car dealership than elsewhere and certainly with bigger dollar implications. Paul Valery said "Our most important thoughts are those which contradict our emotions"[7] and never was it more true from a financial standpoint than at the car dealership.

Over the years, I have met a number of people who get excited about buying, owning, cleaning and driving their cars. I have to admit, I don't get it. I know almost nothing about cars and how they work and while a new car is nice, it doesn't register very high on my list of kicks which may put me in the minority.

There are lots of reasons, some even valid ones, for purchasing a car. On the other hand, I'd like to offer a few of the less compelling arguments I have heard: "I had no choice", "they made me the greatest deal", "I need the depreciation (for those in business)", "I wasn't even in the market for a car but the dealer/my sister/my friend had to get rid of this car", "I wanted to wait a while but the dealer told me there were a lot of other people interested", "I had to move fast

---

7 John Shanahan, *The Most Brilliant Thoughts of All Time*, Harper Collins Publishers, 1999, P. 143

as this was the last one on the lot", and finally, the old standby, "I just got my tax refund and had the down payment".

Financially you should buy a car when your reasoned best conclusion is that after considering the facts, it is necessary or prudent for you to do so now rather than later. Sometimes the facts make the decision clear, other times not so much but recognizing that a new or different car can be an emotional kick, factor this in to the decision and be as objective as you can.

My observation is that frequently there are two alternate and recurring emotional responses that are often intrinsic in the car buying ritual, both of which should be avoided in my opinion. The first is the status or high that is associated with a car that is cool, expensive, rare or we otherwise believe tends to convey some message . The other is the dorky or loser image that may be associated with a small, efficient, inexpensive or ugly car. If we're honest with ourselves, we are likely not immune from either feeling. You might be aware of them and consider them the extreme ends of a decision making spectrum where you would like to find yourself located somewhere between the middle to dorky end rather than the status end. It is worth considering that a new Porsche parked next to your full time residence camper is your right but not necessarily where you want to be.

Once you decide to buy, while there may not be a lot of science to the process, I would advise you to at least do a little homework first. You might narrow down make and model choices, desired options and target price before you start. Does it sound like I am taking a lot of the fun out of the process right out of the gate? Surely you're not surprised. My point is that being focused on a narrow perspective of choices should eliminate a few of the emotional mine fields out there.

I have been told by dealers that the depreciation or the decline in value of a brand new vehicle can be 20% of the cost of the car the minute you drive it off the lot. If true, buying a brand new car for $30,000 means that a day after you buy it is only worth $24,000. If you keep it for ten years, this is arguably less of an issue but, not surprisingly, we don't keep our cars on average anywhere close to ten years. This is true even in today's horrible economy with tens of millions of Americans out of work. My general approach has routinely been to try to buy a late model used car hoping to avoid as much of the first year depreciation as possible. Only three of the fifteen or so cars purchased in my lifetime were brand new. One was the mustang which has been previously referred to as one of my life's impulse buys. Another was a new Volvo and I can't to this day figure out why I bought it at all and certainly not why I bought a new one. If you're wondering, I was sober and of reasonably sound mind at the time. Less than a week after I bought it I came to my senses, painfully aware that it was much too small for me to be comfortable in for any extended period of time. I dragged myself off to the dealer and threw myself on their mercy but, not surprisingly, they were unsympathetic. While I don't recall the price they offered me to buy it back, I do remember being shocked how much lower it was than I had paid and I ended up trading it in at another dealer and taking the hit. Of course, since then I won't give a Volvo dealership so much as a glance as I drive by even though I know it was me who made the incorrect decision. They just hurt my feelings by not being sympathetic to my stupidity.

> **Things to Think About When Buying A Used Car**
>
> *Kelly Blue Book offers the following as a sampling of things to consider when buying a used car.*
> - *Determine what car is right for you, how much you can afford, and reconcile the two.*
> - *Find out your car's value if you are trading it.*
> - *Get a history and safety report on the proposed purchase.*
> - *Conduct a thorough walk around and test drive.*
> - *Negotiate the best price with the dealer or private party.*

I know you realize that the whole car search and buying experience is gamed. The only way to try to negate the process and even the playing field somewhat is with information and restraint. They know the business and numbers better than we do. Our advantages are few but more powerful. We know what we want and need but most importantly we have the power to say "NO".

Common Cents Saving — Vincent Brown

The optimal outcome for the dealer is to sell the most expensive car at the greatest margin but please be assured that the most important thing to them is to sell you something. They are conditioned to control the flow of information and pricing to you in their language and format which accommodates their narrative. Add in the glossy sales hype about resale values, warranties, safety, maintenance costs, mileage and the amount of other information involved and the decision process can be formidable.

All I can offer is some encouragement and maybe some general guidelines. First, remember that while their first and ultimate goal is to sell you a car, there are some vehicles that the dealership wants to sell a little more than others whether it is last year's model, a slow moving model, an overstock or perhaps a vehicle of a certain color or with some other anomaly. This is true of used as well as new cars. There can be savings associated with these preferences of theirs so be aware of them. Maybe even ask them outright if they can offer you a better deal on one car over another. I offer this knowing that those of you who are serious about your cars are already breaking out in hives just considering possible compromises to your choice of model, color and options but perhaps therapy can help you to overcome this. Remember, it is only going to be your new car for a week or so until it becomes just "your car".

Unless you are really knowledgeable about what cars are worth and a skilled negotiator, avoid limiting yourself by responding to questions like" What's your bottom line?", "What do you need your monthly payment to be?", or "What's it going to take to put you in this car today"? If asked one of these pointed questions I suggest you respond that those are not the questions that are relevant to you; instead repeat that you have narrowed down your search to a few makes and models that you believe fit your criteria. Then tell them that the real question is what is the lowest price they can commit to that is fair to you and to the dealership and what is it going to take for them to do that today.

For the record, I would take any discussion about the sticker price with a grain of salt. Whatever is contained on that piece of paper that is so prominently displayed on the car's window, use it to compare relative value of one vehicle to another and as a guide but don't get carried away. These guys aren't new at this.

Options and extras can add much more than you think to the cost of the vehicle. Try hard to get only what you need. You will save accordingly. Last time I looked, a factory installed GPS increased the cost of the car in the $400-$500 range or more. You can get a good GPS for less than $200, take it from car to car and if it lasts, have it after the car is gone.

The third and last new car I purchased was a few years ago. In keeping with my usual plan, I told them what model I wanted and asked to see what they had in a used car from last year in that model. The redesigned model with the leg room I wanted was only in the second year of production and so they only had one of the year old models in stock. It had 10,000 miles on it. We kind of liked the color and got a price. I indicated that they were advertising that model new for almost $3,000 less. They said sure but this one has extras. Whatever the extras were, it seemed to me that they cost a lot of money and none seemed critical to me. I asked what the price would be on that same model and color new with only the extras I needed on it. It was $2,000 less than the used one. I bought it and had a brand new car (or did for a week until it then become just my car) with everything I needed on it. Did I get a good deal? Who knows? I do believe, though, that based on the research I did, what I wanted, what I saw and the prices I was quoted, I walked away thinking that I had done the most prudent thing for me. When it comes to a car, in fact when it comes to many things, this may be the best we can do. My expectation with this car, as it is with all my cars, is that I will keep it until it no longer has value to me so I was looking for the lowest purchase price possible to spread over the extended period of time I hoped to keep the car.

Unless you have difficulty with your credit, I might suggest that it is not likely to be to your advantage to finance with the dealership. Their interest rate is likely to be higher than you can get elsewhere. If they offer zero per cent or some special financing deal, check it out and consider it of course. Since interest on personal auto loans is not deductible on your personal income taxes this is a possible use of your home equity line of credit if you need to finance the auto purchase. The rate will likely be lower than the auto loan also. I'm sure you know that there are no bargain interest rates on auto loans so if you are one of the lucky people who can manage to pay cash, I would certainly advise it. Like many of you, I certainly couldn't pay cash for my first several cars. Knowing I wanted to though, I resorted to yet another game to get started on the road to a savings bias and my goal of car purchases for cash. After I made my last car payment, I continued to set the monthly payment amount aside in savings and earmarked it to go towards paying for the next one.

Many of my clients used to ask about leasing a car which, as near as I can figure, involves a premise that the car is worth so much now, will be worth less at the end of the lease and if you commit to lease it you are going to pay the difference in that beginning and ending value plus very high interest on that difference for the right to use the car during the lease period. At the end of the lease, you usually have the option to buy the car for what they say it's worth then or turn it in. When you turn it in, you are normally subject to charges if your mileage exceeds some stated amount per year. This can be a deterrent to many leases as it is easy to routinely over drive the mileage allowance. At a minimum, you should consider the cost for excess mileage in your calculation as whether you should buy or lease. The last lease I looked at contained a 12,000 mile allowance per year. It is your responsibility to insure and maintain the leased car the same as if you owned it. In general, from a financial standpoint, leasing seems not to be the best idea. However, as always, there are circumstances where it might make sense. As you may be aware, almost everything about the lease including the down payment, term and annual mileage allowance is totally negotiable with the dealer. They will merely adjust the monthly lease repayment to reflect all of these factors. This fact yet again highlights how non-financial considerations can be so much a part of our financial decision making process.

If you are so into cars and so easily bored that the possibility of your keeping a car more than 3 years is pretty remote, I can almost see that leasing might be attractive. You are never going to be without a monthly payment if you trade every three years anyway. In addition, you never really effectively experience any equity benefit in the cars you buy by keeping them after you stop paying for them. So, it seems to me then, that the question becomes how does the lease payment (plus potential extra mileage charges) compare to the installment loan payment you would have paid by purchasing the car? It bears repeating that I still think this is a bad idea from a financial standpoint but may be the lesser of possible evils if you insist on a three or four year cycle for your vehicle fix.

In another scenario, you may be strapped, have little cash to invest in a down payment and need a family car. You can lease a car with a much smaller initial cash payment. The lease payment may result in enough savings compared to the note payment on a purchase that it makes a crucial difference in your cash flow. After three or four years, when the lease is up, you may be able to better afford the payment if you elect to purchase it at the reduced value then or you may be in such an improved financial situation that you can then purchase another car

Again, no one size fits all but it seems to me that the most savings efficient and cost effective way to have a car is to buy it, for cash if you are able to do so, and keep it for as long as possible which may be until reliability or maintenance costs become major factors. In addition, while traversing the buying process even though you will be bombarded with glitzy choices at every turn, and are thinking that you work hard and deserve to treat yourself, and you only live once, try to keep in mind that your initial objective may likely have been practical transportation not a status symbol. At least be conscious of the emotional forces at work. And for heaven's sake, let me state the most obvious and simple of all car buying guidelines. Be willing to walk away. Be willing to say no. Be willing to go to sleep without having bought. The number of people who are called by the dealership after they get home, the next morning or in a few days with a better deal than they left the dealership with is substantial. It has happened to me more than once.

One of the recurring themes of this book is planning or at least making some attempt at objective reflection on your choices before the fact. I know how difficult it can be to struggle to make the best long-term choice when you are "in the moment" with the family all riled up and your "choice" buds tuned in to "I want" instead of "Do I need?" My hope for you is that you commit to do as much prioritizing as you are comfortable doing before the fact; that is before a decision is made to do something whether you are purchasing a car or something else. Either way, once you make your decision not only live with it, but attempt to enjoy it. Tomorrow is another day and your life is never enriched by beating yourself up about things that are over and can't be undone. To me these are not conflicting messages. If I have learned anything over my career about working with people's financial health it is to respect the human factor in all of us.

Gambling

We may disagree as to whether this is a topic worthy of mention and if so, whether it merits its' own chapter. We have repeatedly referred to examples of non-financial considerations crashing into our well-ordered and logical financial landscape. This is one of the biggies. It is also one of those issues that will be either irrelevant or critical to you depending on who you are. Look at it this way, if it's irrelevant the chapter is short. If it's critical, another perspective may help. Additionally, if gambling is not something that hampers your saving efforts, there may be something else that does. My comments are not geared to "compulsive or problem gamblers" but to all of you for whom gambling, or a similar activity, is at least a hobby. If you fall into the compulsive or problem gambler category, then anything I say will likely be woefully inadequate to your needs. This won't take long so let's get to it.

I have loads of relatives and friends who have spent a lot of time in and around casinos and gambling in general. I accompany them occasionally. Being the accountant (it is often alleged that this is a code word for nerd) that I am, I have even read several books on gambling that touched on strategies, betting systems, money management at the table and other gambling related "how to" topics. Many of the books related to craps simply because it is my preferred game. I find it more lively than most of the alternatives, it moves quickly (less down time) and for me offers a fairly short term commitment in time to the point of success or failure. Craps, at least if you stick to the basic proposition bets, is also one of the games that offers the least advantage to the house, though still an advantage. In other words, it gives you a slightly better mathematical chance of winning than other casino games. In keeping with the theme here, I am compelled to state the obvious, namely that the house advantage, no matter how small, is still the house advantage meaning that logically and mathematically, over the long haul, you will lose more than you win.

Some gamblers believe they are going to win every time they play. In fact, I know several people personally who claim exactly that. Others are less optimistic or alternatively, more realistic and some are hopelessly sure that they are destined to lose every dollar they wager. Some gamble on a weekly basis and others only occasionally, some are passionate about it while others are less so. For myself, I am indifferent and could live with it or without it, leaning slightly towards living without it. This may help you put some perspective to my comments but rest assured that I am very aware that it is a source of pleasure for many of us.

First, it is an obvious fact and one accepted even by professional gamblers that you will not win all the time, in fact not even most of the time. The gist of virtually all of my reading on the subject indicates that regardless of your game, mathematical skill and system, you will not win consistently. The professional gamblers, who are better at it and more knowledgeable than we are, may, and I do mean may, end up winning over the long haul. If they do, their success is likely achieved by employing their knowledge and experience, sound judgment, scientific mastery of the odds of success in given situations, a conservative betting system, knowing when to quit and good money management skills.

Every game, horserace and slot machine in every casino or elsewhere is *designed* to favor the house. Some games, like craps (if you restrict yourself to certain basic bets) and blackjack (assuming you know the math) yield only a slight advantage to the house but even then, it is a fact that all things being equal the longer you play, the more they win. And this assumes that you know the rules cold, understand the odds, aren't distracted, make all the right choices and generally stay sober and unaffected by outside influences like your impending divorce, losing your dog or being stalked by an old flame. To repeat, if you do all that you are supposed to do exactly right all the time, you can reduce the house's edge as much as possible to minimize the amount you lose and they win. Sounds pretty inviting doesn't it? Let's not even address the ridiculous odds against you when betting on horses, dogs, jai-alai or God forbid, keno and the lottery. If you are a fan of the poker tournaments on television, it is apparent how difficult it is for even the most skilled players to consistently be successful. No matter how good you are, the odds (I call it reality) are against you and to be successful at any gambling endeavor for the vast majority of us is purely a matter of chance.

But that is the key for so many of us, isn't it? It's the element of chance. It's the thought that we can beat the odds; end up a winner; experience a windfall, get an emotional high. And yes, it is theoretically possible for any of us to walk into a casino, drop $100 on a number and win. In addition, there is the social aspect of the activity. There's nothing wrong with that of course. So here, plain and simple is my take on gambling, not philosophically or morally, but in

A Few Gambling Facts

The following was provided by the Las Vegas Convention and Visitors Authority for the 1996 year.

- *Over 60% of American adults gambled in some way last year.*
- *87% of the 29.6 million people who visited Las Vegas in 1996 gambled.*
- *The average gambling budget per person, per trip was $580.90 and gamblers averaged four hours per day on the activity.*
- *Two decades ago, two states allowed gambling and 48 states outlawed it. In 1996, 48 states had some form of legal gambling. Utah and Hawaii are the two that don't.*
- *Gambling is a $40 billion a year industry in the United States.*

relation to your plan to integrate a savings bias into your life. That is, after all, what we are trying to do here.

If you are not a professional or even a highly skilled and disciplined amateur who knows the numbers, odds and risk elements inside out, don't kid yourself. You are not going to win all, or even most of the time. The facts and mathematics of the whole process are against you and indicate that, subject to your best efforts, the longer you do it, the more you will lose. Chance, luck, alcohol and camaraderie may result in your having some very happy and successful forays into the casinos and I hope that this is the case. There may even be some who admire your continuing to be optimistic about your chances despite the odds. Nevertheless, my thoughts about allocating your hard earned money to gambling are similar to those for other potential uses of your available cash.

I suggest that if you enjoy it and choose to do it as one of the entertainment options in your life, go for it. Provide some allowance in your entertainment budget for it. Spend as much as you are comfortable spending, *but decide in advance how much that is* per trip, per month or whatever and have a blast. I believe that this is what many people do to manage gambling in their life. What is important here is what priorities you have set for yourself and how effective you are managing them.

On those occasions when you win, you might consider taking a substantial portion of your winnings to set aside in your savings, or alternatively to set aside for future gambling activities, leaving more of your other recurring income available for saving.

It doesn't need to be said, but if gambling is an issue for you or if you are not willing to commit to a definitive amount of your funds that you will spend on this activity, then you should reconsider whether you are able to be truly committed to saving in general. Being unwilling to restrict yourself in some way for any of your expenditures is at odds with the mindset I am trying to suggest here. Given the choice of whether to provide growth and financial security to yourself and family in the future through a serious savings plan or from your gambling efforts, it doesn't seem complicated at all. If gambling is a part of your life, budget for it, cap the amount you are willing to spend at it and enjoy it. To let it be any more than that for you is, well it's just a gamble.

One last thought. As I have said, if you gamble, enjoy it within the framework I have suggested above but make every effort not to kid yourself about it. Whether you indulge twice a week or once a year, on any given day your chances of being successful are identical when you walk through the door. If you go more often, it will cost you more. Yes, if you go often, you will mathematically have more profitable days than the once a year visitor but the once a year visitor doesn't experience the multiple days of losses that you will. And to be brutally honest, recurring visits with the expectation that if you go often enough you will hit the big one, while I don't claim it's impossible, is not something any of us should risk our financial security on.

So You Think You Need Some Outside Help

For me, it is usually apparent when I am in a situation where I need help. There are a few things I know a little about and a lot of things that I know almost nothing about and I am pretty clear as to which is which. Occasionally, though, I am convinced that I know what I am doing when I start something only to find reality lurking right around the bend. For that reason, I am offering the following information should you feel stuck.

If you feel you need to seek help with any of the concepts in this book, there are several options available to you, not surprisingly some with better opportunities for success than others, but all generally offering expertise in most of the topics we have discussed. If you are feeling the need for help I encourage you to find it. By now you should be fully aware that I believe strongly in what you are trying to do here and want to do all that I can to help you to stay the course.

The assistance I am talking about will likely be related to questions about your personal record keeping, budgeting, tax planning or tax preparation. Generally, the place you are likely to find sufficient expertise in all of these areas in one place is an accounting or CPA firm. Since it is an industry that I have a history with,

I believe that I can offer some guidance as to when and how such a firm might be helpful to you. First, let's talk a little about tax preparation, not because it is critical to the savings concept but because it is a subject relevant to everyone and again, it is a subject I am familiar with.

I have been asked by clients many times over the years as to whether I thought they could prepare their own tax returns. I routinely responded with a few questions. Do you like puzzles? Do you frustrate easily? Do you think it would be fun? Why are you doing it? If your primary motivation is to save the tax preparation fee, unless you have a very simple tax situation, my advice is simple. Don't do it. Consider doing your own tax return if it is a challenge that appeals to you in some way, if taxes are something you are interested in, or if some part of you thinks it might be fun and will give you a kick knowing you did it yourself and learned a little bit about income taxes. Otherwise, you run the very real risk that it will be more trouble and frustration than it's worth, more than you bargained for and certainly not worth whatever fee you saved. I emphasize the behavioral implications because, in keeping with the theme here, these are the factors that are likely to drive success or failure with the process. As to whether you have or can acquire the needed skills to make sure you do right by yourself, my assumption is that if you enjoy the process and plan it properly you will likely be successful in completing your return correctly and not leaving major tax savings on the table .If you do make the decision to try your return yourself,

---

Tax Software

The 2013 Online Tax Software Review compiled surveys on most major tax software programs available for non-professional preparers.

The programs were rated on a scale of 1 to 10 and the five highest rated programs were:

- *Turbo Tax (10.0),*
- *TaxAct (9.48),*
- *H & R Block (9.13),*
- *TaxSlayer (8.58), and*
- *eSmart Tax (8.25).*

As you can see all are pretty comparable.

These and other programs are readily available and cost from around $10 to $100, including the state return, and must be purchased each year.

only do so by buying and becoming familiar with one of the many computer tax preparation programs out there. They are generally affordable and non-technical in their interface, asking you, for example, if you worked for someone rather than if you had a form W-2. Also, If you continue with the same program each year, you will become more familiar with how it works and your information will automatically carry forward from year to year saving you time and increasing the accuracy of the return.

Do a little research on the programs available and, if possible, talk to people who have used them. Having a friend or relative who has used the program you select is a real plus and may give you the confidence you need to get started not to mention a source for questions that need answers. My limited experience with tax programs designed for non-professionals was with Turbo Tax and I found it worked fine but I have no reason to believe that there aren't others out there that will suit your needs. If you do decide to take the plunge, when your return is complete consider having someone you trust and who is knowledgeable about taxes look it over even if you have to pay for the service, at least for the first year. Organize your data, start early and address questions as they come up so that you educate yourself and again I suggest you try and make a game of it. Don't get discouraged. Initially, everything may seem complex and unintelligible but if you take the issues one at a time you will surprise yourself. Many tax issues, seemingly complex to a novice, are not always so and there is a significant library of free information available for you to work with. You may even have people in your circle of friends and family who like this stuff and are more than happy to share their knowledge with you. As always, the burden is on you to be careful. I can't tell you how many times people have insisted that dog food for their pets was deductible if their pets were guard pets, that bananas were deductible if your doctor suggested more potassium or that the value of the time they spent getting their tax data together was deductible. Generally speaking, none of these are correct, by the way.

On the other hand, be prepared for the reality that until we simplify the tax system and/or go to a flat tax or something similar, depending on your personality and life skills, preparing your return yourself may not be without its' challenges, especially if your situation is a little complex. The tax programs on the market don't eliminate the need to face the issue of what is deductible and what isn't but they will help steer you to the right questions and it certainly takes away any math and calculation issues as the programs do all of the calculations and generally puts everything on the return in the right place. Remember, people less intelligent than you are have learned how to do it and you ultimately control the process.

Excuse me for taking the liberty of inserting a personal comment here for the benefit of all of the tax preparers out there. Several times during the hectic final throws of filing season I received calls in the office from people I didn't know (and obviously weren't clients and didn't intend to become clients) who had questions about something they ran across in preparing their own return. They either didn't know or didn't care that this was how I made my living and apparently assumed that I would be happy to find time in my sixteen hour work day to bring them up to speed on a last minute issue that they had months to resolve and do so free of charge. Simply put, if you take on the preparation of your return, do your own homework and if you need outside help be respectful of other people's time and if you solicit help from a professional, be prepared to pay for the assistance you need or at least to gracefully acknowledge the help.

Whether you do it yourself, or use a preparer, take this small bit of advice. Address the gathering of your data and the filing of your returns sooner rather than later. You may think you work better under pressure but it's my belief that, in most things, the best results are seldom achieved when you are rushed. In addition, if you have issues or questions, knowing about them earlier is always better. If you have a preparer do it, they routinely prepare them in the order they are received in their office. Consider whether you would prefer that your return be prepared in February rather than April 14 at 3:00 a.m. when preparers have been at it hard for seven days a week, 14 to 16 hours a day for three months and are in crunch mode. It also goes without saying that if you have someone else do your return, you will be responsible for gathering and submitting accurate and complete data to them. You are doing yourself a disservice if you throw a box of stuff at them thinking they will do better for you than you would, not to mention that it will cost you in higher fees. Being aware enough to get your own input together also goes along with my theory that all of us need to know enough about what our tax situation is to be able to manage it effectively. If you hear anything I say, hear that you are not helpless here. It is very manageable.

Now back to seeking outside help. Whether you are looking to secure the services of someone to do your taxes or to help you with your budget, an accounting program or other financial issues, there is a boutique of choices out there. Before we talk about the differences in the choices, here are a few general thoughts. When securing the services of any professional, it is a given that you should do your due diligence to determine that they have the required expertise and professionalism to provide the needed services. Given that, the next most important element of any professional relationship is chemistry. To me chemistry means trust, the ability to communicate, mutual honesty and a general comfort level between professional and client in working together. Whether you engage an individual or a large firm, don't kid yourself. It is all about how you feel about the individual who will be one on one with you. Crunching the numbers is a commodity you can buy from most preparers. Someone who listens to and understands you, takes satisfying you seriously and believes that their job is to present options is not a commodity. The most expensive professional need not be the most astute; more importantly the best or most sophisticated service is not necessarily the best for you. Be realistic about what your needs are.

If it is not already obvious to you, consider that there are significant differences in the competency and level of dedication among accountants and tax preparers. As you would suspect, some are smarter than others, some work harder than others and as in any business, professionals develop expertise with those issues they run into most often. A good accountant should know, or can easily find out, whatever information is needed to effectively address any tax or other issue you may have but reality is reality. For example, a small accountant in New York City may not be the best choice if you need expertise in farming. Similarly, an accountant in Maine will have less familiarity with a State of California tax return than he will for a Maine return. It's also a fact that being able to find the answers to a question you don't deal with every day assumes that your advisor has the time, inclination and resources to do so.

So what types of accountant or tax preparer should you use? Here are some thoughts presented with the full disclaimer that they are opinion and necessarily general in nature. The duty to check out individual alternatives rests with you. Most communities have tax preparers who run businesses out of their homes or small offices, sometimes a sideline business with some other activity engaged in for profit after filing season. If the image of your preparer sitting on his couch in his briefs with his laptop in front of him watching American Idol with a plate of nachos and a beer and your tax information spread out beside him is disconcerting to you, this may be a red flag. There is no requirement for these preparers to meet minimum standards, keep proficient in law changes, or adhere to any ethical standards. They are busy trying to make a living, may not have a lot of accounting expertise and may do tax returns only for 3-4 months a year. As to how effective they are in the process, how sophisticated their tax software is, what subscriptions they pay for and maintain to update tax reference materials, whether or not they attend tax courses, these are questions I can't answer. For the record, I can't imagine that there are any tax preparers anywhere that don't purchase a professional computer program to do tax returns. If you somehow run across a preparer who gives you a return prepared by hand, a return done with carbon paper, or a return that just looks tacky in general, be afraid. Be very afraid.

Another concern I have with at home part time preparers, other than the fact that they may have no accounting expertise, is that there is normally no one else to review their work. Not only does an independent review avoid clerical and input errors but, more importantly it subjects your return to another preparer professional who may offer savings or planning ideas, or note obvious missing items on your return that the primary preparer missed. I know that large CPA firms put all returns through an extensive review process. When I was in practice in my small firm, I insisted on it. I cannot assure you that all small preparers do a review. It is a legitimate question to ask.

Are some of these preparers adequate? Surely, some are but my advice is that they should only be used if you believe you know the preparer pretty well and trust their level of dedication. They might also not be the best source of support for your needs outside of the area of tax preparation.

The next upgrade for tax preparation services are, in my view, the large franchise preparers that you see advertising all over the place during tax season or hawked by someone in costume holding a sign on the side of a road near you. Their names are known to you and their advertising promises that they won't make any mistakes, will take advantage of every deduction, will review returns other people have prepared and likely amend those returns to get you money back and on and on. The first thing to know is that, they are not as inexpensive as you might think. Published data for the 2012 year indicates that H & R Block's average fee was $192 and the average at Liberty Tax was $173. These averages may be skewed if a large portion of the returns done by these firms are very simple returns which I suspect is the case.

In addition, for these preparers, everything they do is standardized. It is all done by checklist. The more they guarantee that nothing will ever be questioned on your return, the more you can assume that they are likely to be over cautious which I contend is not always a good thing no matter how conservative you are. I believe they make an effort to get good people, make sure that they have good basic knowledge of simple tax issues, and you will likely end up with an accurately prepared return. That means they will place what you give them on the correct line of the return and all calculations will be accurate. While this is certainly not a bad thing, it may be seriously lacking in the areas of planning ideas and encouraging you to maximize your deductions and reduce your tax liability. Don't take any comfort in anyone's guarantee that your return will be clerically accurate. That should be a given. It's like bragging about not beating your kids. Accuracy is math and a computer is crunching all the numbers. We all want our tax returns to be "clean" and fly under the radar but I think it is a legitimate (and necessary) exercise to ask ourselves to what extent we are willing to go to assure it. Your return needs to be accurate but not at the cost of failing to take an aggressive position on legitimate issues. Since these franchises do tax preparation almost exclusively, they would not routinely have expertise in other accounting and financial areas if you are seeking it.

> **Tax Preparation Fees**
>
> *The National Association of Accountants indicates that for a recent year, the average fee for a federal and state personal tax return with itemized deductions was $246, and for a federal and state return without itemized deductions was $143.*
>
> *Additional forms, if required, increased the cost of the return but not significantly.*
>
> *These averages are reported primarily from one-person operations and smaller firms.*

I am biased in believing that you should be looking for advice, creativity, and an honest assessment of options both in the tax and financial area. My experience confirms, without question, that some of the tax rules, especially as they relate to businesses are subject to interpretation. No one should ever suggest that you cheat or lie. If they do, get rid of them. A good preparer should however, encourage you to manage your tax situation to the extent possible as well as consider your other needs and your lifestyle.

The other, and to my thinking the best, source of help are accounting firms ranging from one person firms to international organizations with thousands of employees.

Some are firms of certified public accountants, others are not. The rules for becoming a Certified Public Accountant (CPA) vary slightly by State but generally require an accounting degree and passing an extensive standardized five part exam. As a CPA, almost all States require that you take a certain number of hours (normally 40) each year in course training designed to keep your skills current. You must furnish proof of your work to renew your certificate. CPA's also have State boards and societies that provide training, materials and support to practicing CPA's as well as an outlet for clients who have negative experiences. Accountants who are not certified may not be degreed in accounting or anything else for that matter and are not required to take any courses or training on an annual basis. Does this mean that they are not as smart or capable? Certainly not, it means what it means, namely that they are not regulated at all as to qualifications or skills.

These full time accounting firms normally charge for their services by the hour whereas the other groups of preparers more routinely charge by the number of schedules prepared or some other fixed cost schedule. The accounting firms normally do other things besides income taxes but many of these firms, especially the smaller ones are heavily weighted with tax work. Other services might include auditing, accounting support, bookkeeping and other specialized accounting needs. They obviously could help you with many of the things we have discussed in this book. Many of them are also usually proficient with QuickBooks. In fact, many of my clients brought their QuickBooks files to me to use in their tax preparation. Because they are full time professionals, they are available all year, and should endeavor to use their knowledge of your tax situation to provide personalized planning, advice and support.

Hourly rates will vary by geographic location, size of the firm and other issues. Some firms have minimum fees for tax preparation but any firm should give you an estimate, perhaps even a fixed price for a given year, for your work after taking a look at your situation. If you have a business, or other issues complicating your financial picture, I believe that when it comes to engaging a tax preparer, a full time accounting firm is definitely appropriate for you. Remember, they are not all equally competent and certainly you will not have chemistry with all of them. Find a firm that offers you an individual you like and trust, ask him or her to commit to being your contact for as long as you are with the firm, talk about fees up front and ask what you can do to keep fees reasonable. These full timers will likely result in higher costs, but the firm's value to you will be in the tax planning and advice it provides not just in the return preparation.

It's important to me that you believe that taking on the tasks dealt with in this book are well within your grasp despite a lack of accounting or financial acumen. This includes preparing your own tax return if you take the job on for the right reasons. At the same time I want to assure you that there are always resources available to you if you need help. My intention in writing this, however, was to suggest things that most of us could do on our own without involving outside professionals.

A Few Final Thoughts

One of the first admissions I made to you was that nothing in these pages was profound. The more time I spent in putting my thoughts together, the more I considered whether suggesting such a simplistic concept for creating a mindset for managing your financial life would be of value to you. Note that I acknowledge my own advice and admit that simplistic does not mean easy. Further, even if it was of value, could it easily be applied to your particular situation in your life considering the diversity of our backgrounds, education and personality and those of our spouses and family members who need to be part of your plan? In the end, I concluded that it is the reality of all of these diverse influences on your life that might make my suggestions helpful and perhaps even necessary. My hope was to offer some clarity, guidance and encouragement to what may be, for some, a difficult day to day process.

Whatever I did or did not do well in my life up until now, I know that my remaining years are going to be as good as I can make them based on the choices I have made along the way. Hopefully, you now have some of the tools that will help you in your process to build your future. Let me once again and for the last time state the obvious.

You only have so much time to prepare yourself for anything, retirement included. That is fact, not a slogan. Don't fall into the trap of doing nothing simply because you feel you can't do it all. If you can't do a lot, be content with doing a little. I am convinced that doing a little as often as you can is always preferable to doing a lot once or twice and infinitely better than doing nothing. Forming the habit of saving and bringing planning and priority setting to your daily decision making process will yield substantially more benefit than hoping that some future stroke of luck or event will fix it all for you.

If you are younger and starting out it certainly may be more difficult for you to set money aside but it's the perfect time to start making saving at least a small part of your life and you have the biggest advantage of all on your side, time. If you are middle aged, you may be in the perfect place to adopt a saving bias as you may be somewhat established, your kids are on in years, you are likely to have a little more disposable income and you still have time left to affect a difference. If you are approaching retirement, of course you have less time to make it happen but likely fewer obligations and certainly more motivation. It is better to start late than never start at all and this could be the first big project of your future retirement planning.

By now the point should be obvious. The train that is your life will arrive at your later years ahead of schedule. On the trip, do what little you can when you can to make it easier later. Do not let yourself get discouraged. The mere act of trying to make it a priority in your life puts you way ahead of a lot of folks. Finally, you will never be sorry for having made the effort to save and the one thing you don't need me to tell you is that it won't happen unless you decide that it will.

Every one of us, regardless of our intelligence, education, wealth or the luck we have had or not had in life is very similar in our thinking in some very basic ways. We tend to find it difficult to dwell on the good things in our life. In those quiet moments our thoughts tend to settle on those life issues we wish were different and we would like to change. One of those issues is our basic desire for security

Common Cents Saving   **Vincent Brown**

and some measure of independence. In our efforts to create this security and independence every last one of us will struggle with choices of what we and our family want now and the knowledge that for each of these choices there is a cost and impact on our future. If I have made some impression on you, you will accept this fact and not avoid or deny it. You will deal with it and not dismiss it. If you accept and deal with this basic human issue, you may win some of your battles and be much better poised to enjoy your life after the war.

Chapter Highlights

The following is a quick recap of the major points I tried to make in each chapter of this book.

The Proposition

Life is short. For some of us times are tough and the future may be less predictable than ever. Your ability to secure the best possible future for yourself is in your own hands and will be best served by adopting a committed plan to save and using some simple tools to implement and nourish it and by making it a comfortable part of your working life. We have to recognize that doing so may require that we think a little differently about things than we have in the past.

To Save or Not to Save

Wanting to save is not enough. Saving must be planned and made a real part of your day to day life without interfering negatively with it. Savings includes setting aside a predetermined amount of money from each paycheck into a separate account, trying to make sound financial decisions on a day to day basis, making an effort to avoid impulse purchases, avoiding abuse of credit cards and managing waste in your life. The success of these efforts will very likely be determined more by your commitment to them than by whether or not you know how to do them.

Will a Budget Help?

One of the major elements of a savings plan is being able to determine a specific amount of your pay that you estimate will be able to be set aside for savings. Preparing a budget is one good way of attempting to calculate that amount. A budget, or similar exercise, will require a historical summary of your prior transactions and critical assessment of potential future ones. The psychological advantage to this process is significant because it requires you to make tough objective decisions, albeit tentative ones, in advance and free of the emotional influences of real time decision making.

Improving Your Tax IQ

Few of us will ever be tax experts. Even if we're not, you are responsible for your own tax return and some elementary knowledge of what it contains is helpful and gives you valuable insight into managing your tax situation and maximizing your savings. Every tax return, regardless of its' complexity or the level of income, is summarized on the two pages of the main tax form, Form 1040 which contains only five or six major categories of income, deductions and payments. You should have a general understanding of the form, how it works and where the numbers come from.

Banking

Generally banks are commodities offering similar services and the choice of one over another is not likely to affect our savings directly. Choose one that is convenient and allows easy access to free checking and on line bill payment. Try and qualify for a home equity line of credit to use when needed and avoid those excessive bank charges that cost you so dearly.

Kids and Family - You Gotta Love 'Em

For all of us, especially if you have children, it is a given that our family will play a major role in how our assets are accumulated and utilized. There are no "rules" for these almost always emotional choices. Therefore, it is important that you make an effort to think about these issues before they arise, consider alternatives, make preliminary judgments and communicate them to family members. This will help to assure that everyone will at least start out on the same page and you will be as prepared as possible to face the rigors of your families' emotional and financial needs.

Retirement Plans

Contributions to qualified retirement plans should be funded before savings whenever possible and are generally superior to putting aside after tax dollars primarily because of the tax benefits of contributions and earnings. To the extent that you can, maximize your qualified retirement plan contributions at least to the extent that they produce current tax benefit and/or take advantage of matching contributions from your employer.

Vacations, Toys and Other Goodies

To be effective, the amount of your savings goal must reflect what is available after your ongoing operating costs including reasonable estimates for fun and leisure. It's not enough to be smart and rich. You also need to be effective and happy. The extent and cost of your leisure is one of those tough decisions involving weighing current gratification against the opportunity for future choices. Your ability to have those choices in your later years will likely be more important to you than you think it will be now.

Homes and Cars: Life's Major Purchases

Purchase of a home or a car is a part of our financial lives. Buying a home in the current economy involves the consideration of negative consequences that didn't have to be considered in the past. Appreciation can't be guaranteed; in fact we have learned that values can decline on an annual basis. Turnover of real estate for profit is not a sure thing and requires much more time than it used to take. In addition, job security and the economy are shaky. Simply put, ownership of real estate deserves much more caution than it did and needs to be looked at a little differently. As to buying cars, consider the emotional aspects of the process, buy only when you have to, consider only what you need and keep the vehicle for as long as possible to minimize overall vehicle cost. For those of you who are intimately involved with your vehicles, well... do the best you can.

Gambling

To my way of thinking gambling is entertainment but with potentially significant differences The amount you spend on gambling is often determined on impulse, at the moment without a great deal of thought. It can be open ended and may not be limited by the amount of the cash in your pocket or the credit limit on your charge card. Finally, the amount you are willing to spend on gambling can be artificially justified by an exaggerated expectation of winning, a concept not usually present with other entertainment choices. If you enjoy it, budget for it and treat it the same as your other entertainment. Use your head, set your limits beforehand and manage your winnings if you are lucky enough to experience them. If gambling is a problem for you, address it and make it a priority that supersedes any efforts at saving or other long-term planning.

So You Think You Need Outside Help

Most of you can be successful with the tools provided in this book on your own. However, If you are looking for some guidance or support in the areas of budgeting, record keeping, retirement planning, tax planning or tax preparation, there are many options open to you. Full-service accounting or CPA firms are a good option as you can get help with all of these needs in one place and establish a relationship with someone who can work with you all year and on an ongoing basis.

A Few Final Thoughts

All of us have our own course to chart in life with no guarantee of what we will face in the future. What is common to all of us is that we would like to be prepared for life's surprises and emergencies, and have as much flexibility as we can when we retire. You have only a limited amount of time to prepare to make it happen and there is no possibility of going back to change what we have done or haven't done in the past. You will never regret the efforts you have made today for a better tomorrow. I hope that I have helped provide you with some of the tools and the motivation to make that effort for yourself.

Acknowledgments

As this was my first literary venture, my very low expectations were surpassed only by my inexperience and lack of knowledge of how the literary world works. The whole process was navigable only because of the encouragement I got from family and friends.

Thanks to my wife Mary, my first and primary proofreader who never met a family member who wasn't perfect; my oldest son Chris for the cover design and his creative and unique insight into life; my youngest son Dominic who is my expert on all things literary and has the blessed ability to let you know you got it all wrong in such a way you love him for it; Melissa for her upbeat, quirky and zealous input; and to other family members who interrupted their lives to help.

Thanks to David Minter, my outside literary expert who read the book while recovering from a debilitating accident; Ken Karofsky, my biggest fan; and Peter Hoffman who shocked me by offering page-by-page input. Thank you all for taking the time to read it. More importantly, thanks for encouraging me that this information may help people in a unique way. Finally, thanks to Rick Richolson for relieving me of all my concerns about the technicalities of publishing a work.

www.ingramcontent.com/pod-product-compliance
Lightning Source LLC
Chambersburg PA
CBHW051725170526
45167CB00002B/797